HOW TO TEACH AI

Weaving Strategies and Activities Into Any Content Area

Rachelle Dené Poth

International Society for Technology in Education
ARLINGTON, VA

How to Teach AI
Weaving Strategies and Activities Into Any Content Area
Rachelle Dené Poth

Senior Acquisitions Editor: *Valerie Witte*
Developmental Editor: *Linda Laflamme*
Copy Editor: *Linda Laflamme*
Proofreader: *Lisa Hein*
Indexer: *Valerie Haynes Perry*
Book Design and Production: *Danielle Foster*
Cover Design: *Masie Chong*

Library of Congress Cataloging-in-Publication Data
Names: Poth, Rachelle Dené, author.
Title: How to teach AI : weaving strategies and activities into any content area / Rachelle Dené Poth.
Description: First edition. | Arlington, VA : International Society for Technology in Education, [2024]. | Includes bibliographical references.
Identifiers: LCCN 2024012018 (print) | LCCN 2024012019 (ebook) | ISBN 9798888370353 (paperback) | ISBN 9798888370339 (epub) | ISBN 9798888370346 (pdf)
Subjects: LCSH: Artificial intelligence—Study and teaching. | Interdisciplinary approach in education.
Classification: LCC Q335.7 .P67 2024 (print) | LCC Q335.7 (ebook) | DDC 006.3071/2—dc23/ eng/20240509
LC record available at https://lccn.loc.gov/2024012018
LC ebook record available at https://lccn.loc.gov/2024012019

First Edition
ISBN: 979-8-88837-035-3
Ebook version available

Printed in the United States of America

ISTE® is a registered trademark of the International Society for Technology in Education.

About ISTE

The International Society for Technology in Education (ISTE) is a nonprofit that brings together a passionate community of global educators. Our vision is that all students engage in transformative learning experiences that spark their imagination and prepare them to thrive in learning and life. ISTE's mission is to empower educators to reimagine and redesign learning through impactful pedagogy and meaningful technology use. We achieve this by offering transformative professional learning, fostering vibrant communities, and ensuring that digital tools and experiences are accessible and effective.

Related ISTE Titles

AI in the Classroom: Strategies and Activities to Enrich Student Learning
By Nancye Blair Black

Chart a New Course: A Guide to Teaching Essential Skills for Tomorrow's World
By Rachelle Dené Poth

AI for School Leaders: 62 Ways to Lighten Your Workload and Focus on What Matters
By Vickie F. Echols

To see all books available from ISTE, please visit iste.org/books.

About the Author

DR. RACHELLE DENÉ POTH is an edtech consultant, presenter, attorney, author, and longtime educator with more than six years of experience teaching about, presenting on, and writing about AI. Rachelle teaches Spanish and STEAM: Emerging Technology at Riverview High School in Oakmont, PA. Rachelle has a Juris Doctor degree from Duquesne University School of Law and a Master's in Instructional Technology. She received her second doctorate, focused on Instructional Technology, in May of 2024 from Duquesne University. Her research addressed the need for professional development related to AI for educators.

An ISTE Certified Educator and a Microsoft Innovative Educator Expert, Rachelle is a past-president of the ISTE Teacher Education Network and served on the Leadership team of the Mobile Learning Network for five years. She received the 2017 Outstanding Teacher of the Year award from PAECT (Pennsylvania Association for Educational Communications in Technology, the PA affiliate of ISTE), the 2019 ISTE Making IT Happen Award in 2019, as well as several Presidential gold and silver awards for her volunteer service to education. Rachelle was named one of 30 K–12 IT Influencers for 2021, one of 150 Women Thought Leaders to Follow for 2022, and an EdTech Trendsetter by EdTech Digest for 2024.

Rachelle has written ten books, including *Things I Wish [...] Knew* in which 50 educators from around the world share their thoughts, and is a columnist for Defined Learning, Edutopia, and Getting Smart. In addition to her podcast *ThriveinEDU*, she has hosted the podcast *Practical PBL Strategies by Defined Learning* on the BAM Radio Network.

Rachelle is also a host of *ThriveinEDU* Live and leads a community of educators on Facebook. She presents regularly at state, national, and international conferences and provides professional development and coaching for educators on a variety of topics, including assessments and such emerging technologies as AI, AR, VR, and STEM.

Acknowledgments

Author Acknowledgments

I want to express my gratitude to the ISTE team who provided support as I crafted this book for educators. AI has been a passion of mine for many years, and I am thankful for Valerie Witte for believing in me and Linda Laflamme for supporting me and providing tremendous insight into the development of this book.

I would like to thank my parents for all of the encouragement they've given me as a child and an adult and for always providing opportunities for me to learn, to be curious, and to keep exploring more. There are opportunities everywhere, and my love of learning has been instilled by truly supportive parents who to this day help me to navigate the constantly changing world and remind me of the importance of learning, taking risks, making mistakes, and continuing to grow in my professional practice and personally.

Publisher Acknowledgments

ISTE gratefully acknowledges the contributions of the following:

ISTE Standards reviewers

Frederick Ballew

Mia Gutsell

Tana Ruder

Manuscript reviewers

Heather Brantley

David Lockett

Gwynn Moore

Pattie Morales

Tim Needles

Contents

Chapter 3

The Impact of AI in Education 47

Chapter 4

Putting ChatGPT and GenAI to Work 73

Chapter 5

Fostering Creators and Innovators with AI 97

Introduction

IN TODAY'S DIGITAL AGE, teaching about artificial intelligence (AI) has become an essential component of preparing students for the future. As AI continues to transform various industries, educators have a responsibility to stay current with changes and provide students with the necessary knowledge and skills to succeed in a rapidly changing world and job market.

"Easy for you to say," you may be thinking, "but I'm just a _____ teacher."

I understand!

Exploring new ideas or tools can be challenging. You may feel like you don't have the necessary knowledge, lack a specific skill set, or can't fit it into the curriculum. Sometimes there's barely enough time in your day-to-day or weekly class schedule to cover the basics, let alone "extras" like AI. Back in 2017, I was in the same boat. I dove into the waters of AI without very much knowledge at all, but I knew that I needed to start so that my students would have opportunities to best prepare them for the future. I was surprised to discover how much we already were relying on AI in our daily lives—without necessarily realizing it. Over the years, AI has become an increasingly large focus point for me as an educator and learner; I even made it the focus of my doctoral research. I am still curious to know more about AI and to share how this technology will impact education and the work that we do. For more than six years, I have taught, written about, and presented sessions on AI to students and educators from around the world.

Now my goal is to help *you* realize that teaching about AI is an essential component of preparing students for the future and that the task is not as daunting as you may think. You don't need to have any special qualifications, you just need to start, to dive in. Share your experiences, lead sessions with your colleagues, and even write blogs about it. Have fun learning and exploring! I will help you shift away from saying "I am *just* a _____ teacher" to realizing that you can bring these learning opportunities to your students no matter what your specialty area.

Why Everyone Needs to Teach About AI

As AI continues to transform various industries, educators must stay current with these changes and provide students with the necessary knowledge and skills to succeed in a rapidly changing job market. We have no guarantees of the types of jobs that will exist in the future and how technology will further impact the jobs that exist now. What jobs will not exist in five years, which will rely on AI rather than humans, and what new opportunities will evolve? To ensure they have the flexibility to adapt, our students must exercise critical thinking, creativity, and problem-solving. Working with AI to learn about its benefits, impact, and occasional inaccuracies will give them plenty of opportunities to practice those skills. At the same time, students also will learn about ethics, bias, and the impact of technology on society, which will help them become responsible digital citizens and develop social and emotional learning (SEL) skills.

According to Lee and Perret (2022), "To productively participate in the age of AI, all youth must gain a fundamental understanding about how AI works and how it will impact their lives." At the time they wrote, AI education was facing significant barriers, such as insufficient curriculum available for students in grades K through 12, few training opportunities, and little preparation to offer AI-related learning (Lee & Perret, 2022). At the time I write, just a short two years later, more and more organizations are offering activities and curriculum to help educators rise to the challenge (you'll learn more about these in the chapters that follow).

We know that in order to bring about change, we have to embrace the technology and the risk-taking that comes with it. We all must embrace the new opportunities that arise and figure out how to navigate this world of artificial intelligence for the benefit of our students. It starts with us, so we each have to take that first step whether we want to or not. While you'll face challenges, especially if technology is not a personal strong suit, the task comes with a lot of positives.

How You Can Prepare Yourself

According to Touretzky et al. (2019), an increasing number of teachers are seeking more guidance on how to teach about artificial intelligence, but they lack a background in AI or computer science and, therefore, lack confidence. Don't let this stop you. The only way to gain experience is to try. I assure you that you *can* do it and there *is* time. You can use many quick and simple activities that don't take much time at all: mini-lessons spread throughout the year, quick class discussions, or use of an AI-powered tool and a follow-up reflection. (The book's Try This! icon will point out ideas for you.)

Throughout this book, we will explore the answers to some of your biggest questions, such as:

✦ Why should I bring AI into my _____ classroom?

✦ How do I get started with teaching about AI?

✦ What are the best resources that I can use to get started with it in my classroom, and how do I find them?

✦ How do I prepare my students for the future, especially when we don't know what types of jobs will exist for them?

✦ And, maybe most importantly, how can I ever keep up when technology changes so rapidly?

At almost every session I present, finding time to keep up is one of the biggest worries I hear. It's true, we are surrounded by information with so many blogs, books, podcasts, presentations, and more focused on AI. Even if you could read, watch, or listen to everything, it seems that as soon as a blog or a book is written or a presenter speaks about an AI tool, the next day there's a new feature or a change—or the product disappears entirely. Yes, there will always be changes, improvements, features we love that disappear, and features we are not fond of that we grow to love, but that's just part of the journey—and no excuse not to take that first step.

How This Book Helps

The purpose of *How to Teach AI* is to empower and support all K–12 teachers to become more confident and comfortable integrating AI into their curriculum, regardless of technical background, grade level, or content area taught. My goal is to help you prepare your students with appropriate learning activities and resources that will enable them to understand emerging technologies such as AI and the potential impact on their lives now and in the future.

In the chapters that follow, you will find accessible and practical tools to help you teach about and leverage the power of AI in your instructional practice. We will discuss the foundations of AI, such as algorithms, machine learning, natural language processing, neural networks, and generative AI (including the ubiquitous ChatGPT), and I'll provide examples of how these technologies are being implemented in various industries, as well as their impact on education. The book will also address the ethical and social implications of AI and offer inspiration and resources for how to teach these emerging technologies in the classroom.

By incorporating guided instructions, example activities, and a variety of learning resources, you can create authentic and meaningful experiences that will best prepare students and yourself for the future. The book will serve as a guide for your learning journey by offering lesson ideas, discussion topics, activities, and assessments. Look for two icons as guideposts along the way:

 Try This!

 Activity

When I started teaching about AI in my classroom, I simply learned as I taught, exploring many resources in search of what I thought would be the most impactful for student learning. Finding opportunities to bring to my students, engaging them in conversations, and exploring tools together was *our* path. Sometimes it was a windy path with uncertainty as to answers to students' questions, how to best provide opportunities for students to create and be independent, and finding time for me to learn more.

How to Teach AI stems from my years of experience vetting tools and resources in my classroom, exploring them with students, and learning together. But mine isn't the only voice you'll hear. Educators from across the country will share their experiences teaching and learning AI, as well in the book's "Educator's Perspective" sidebars, which are full of inspiration and easy classroom-tested ideas and activities. Each chapter ends with a summary of core concepts and related ISTE Standards, as well as prompts for reflection and discussion—whether with your inner voice or your colleagues.

The book will give you the guidance and support that you need to get started at any level and in any course. By incorporating guided instructions, example activities, and a variety of learning resources in the classroom, you can create meaningful experiences that will best prepare students and yourself. As your guide to teaching about AI and leveraging

AI-powered tools to enhance your teaching practice, this book will provide you with lesson ideas, discussion prompts, class activities, and assessments. I've also curated a list of AI-powered tools and learning resources that will benefit you and your students in your journey to learn together. You can find a snapshot of this list in Appendix B or by scanning the QR code at the end of each chapter. I'll keep the online list updated as I find more resources and test new tools.

tinyurl.com/ykt7c8z9

My hope is that by the end of this book you will feel confident, excited, and hopeful about AI and its impact in education and the world. Together we can prepare our students for what comes next.

Enjoy your learning journey!

Rachelle

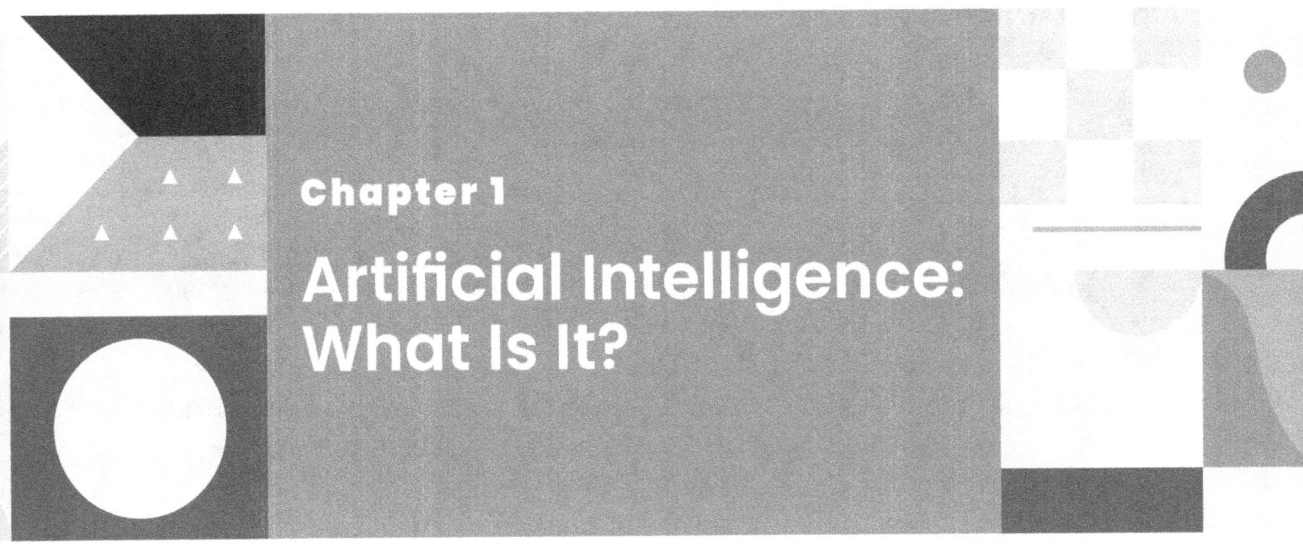

The content of this chapter aligns with the following standards and indicators:

ISTE Student Standards

1.1.d Empowered Learner

1.3.d Knowledge Constructor

1.4.d Innovative Designer

1.5.d Computational Thinker

ISTE Educator Standards

2.1.c Learner

2.2.c Leader

2.3.c Citizen

2.4.b Collaborator

ARTIFICIAL INTELLIGENCE (AI) is not as new as you might think. Following the earlier work of Alan Turing, John McCarthy coined the term back in 1956 in his proposal for the Dartmouth Summer Research Project on Artificial Intelligence, and the use of artificial intelligence in education has been studied for almost 40 years (Crompton et al., 2022). These days, we're all interacting with AI on a daily basis—whether we realize it or not—and many of us are being urged to incorporate it into our classrooms. But how?

To teach about AI, we first need to understand its foundational concepts, basic vocabulary, and impact in our world. This chapter will help you do just that. We will delve into such AI concepts as algorithms, machine learning, natural language processing, and neural networks, as well as discuss examples of them at work in everyday life. By the end of this chapter, you will understand not only the basics of AI, but more importantly, how to engage your students in learning about AI.

What Is AI?

What first comes to mind when you hear the term *artificial intelligence*? C-3PO, R2-D2, and the other *Star Wars* droids? The robots in *I, Robot* developing the capacity to think like humans? The *Terminator* films? When I began presenting on AI, science-fiction characters were the most common answers I heard, from students and educators alike. Years later, voice assistants like Alexa, Cortana, Echo, and Siri began to spring to mind first. AI was becoming less fanciful and more ingrained in ordinary life. Then in late November of 2022, ChatGPT launched publicly, and AI was not only all over the news, but also moved to the forefront in the educational space.

So, what *is* AI?

My simplest, briefest answer is: programs that enable computers to perform actions that have typically been performed by humans. In his proposal for the Dartmouth Summer Research Project, John McCarthy wrote that the researchers, professors, and scientists who attended the gathering were "to proceed on the basis of the conjecture that every aspect of learning or any other feature of intelligence can in principle be so precisely described that a machine can be made to simulate it" (Dartmouth College, 2023). Thanks to those precise descriptions—what we'd now call computer code—AI can process massive amounts of information, recognize images, understand text, generate endless types of content, and do things that would normally require human intelligence and vast amounts of time. AI programs also can learn on their own by making adjustments and improvements based on past iterations, so they then are able to complete even more tasks and very complex ones too.

Just as humans are not all equally capable of the same things, AI comes in multiple types. *Weak* or *narrow* AI performs such tasks as image, voice, and facial recognition. When you use Siri or unlock your phone by looking at it, you're interacting with weak AI. IBM developed Watson, a highly advanced AI system that played a live game of *Jeopardy* with two human opponents in 2011. While it performed incredibly, it was still considered an advanced form of narrow AI. *Artificial general intelligence* (*AGI*) or *strong* AI is capable of understanding, adapting, learning, and creating in ways that are similar to what humans can do. It can understand ideas and languages, problem-solve, reason, and perform intellectual tasks similar to a human. As wide a variety and volume of human-like tasks as AI can accomplish, however, it cannot think and feel like a human. Dr. Helen Crompton, my co-presenter at ISTELive 22, referred to AI as "all head and no heart."

Sometimes it's difficult to realize exactly how much we are interacting with AI in our lives on a daily basis. It enhances our workflow from the use of speech-to-text to save time typing correspondence and documents to quick Google searches that provide access to endless resources when we need them. It impacts our productivity (thank you, email spam filter) and helps in our personal lives in many ways. For example, AI can track our purchases on Amazon or our viewing habits on Netflix and YouTube, learn our preferences from them, and then offer product and entertainment recommendations the next time we visit the site. Similarly, Spotify's DJ Assistant can analyze your favorites and song lists and generate customized playlists in real time. It even talks to you, which is amazing and a bit unnerving at the same time. Sometimes AI suggests songs, videos, or products that may not meet your interests, but that's outweighed by the convenience of having the vast possibilities analyzed for you—far faster than searching yourself.

AI is revolutionizing life in many other ways too. Think about ordering food from a kiosk, automated toll payments on the turnpike, or self-checkout at stores. So many things are now automated, thanks to AI's capability to process information and complete transactions. Some jobs that required humans are now being done by AI (Napolitano, 2023). For this reason, I think it's important for us and for students to understand exactly how much AI is used and relied upon in our world.

As educators, we are in the best position to help our students understand all that they can about artificial intelligence, how it impacts them in everyday life, and how it may impact them in the future. To do so, however, *we* have to understand and continue to learn about AI. A good first step is to become familiar with some of the key terms surrounding it. Knowing the vocabulary related to AI will help you engage in conversations and build your comfort in talking about emerging technologies. When everyone is using the same acronyms, for example, it's easier to understand what you're each referring to. Let's look at some of the key terms related to artificial intelligence: algorithms, generative AI, machine learning, natural language processing, and neural networks.

What Are Algorithms?

Like all computer programs, AI is built on algorithms. An *algorithm* is a set of instructions that a computer has been programmed to follow in order to accomplish a task. The instructions take the form of lines of code. Simple algorithms perform simple jobs; more difficult tasks require more complicated algorithms, and both can be combined to perform extremely complex tasks. The algorithms underlying AI provide instructions that enable it to analyze data, check for spelling and grammar mistakes in text, recognize speech, and much more. Are algorithms always perfect? No, errors can occur that cause unforeseen problems (which is one reason we need to update our phones), and some suffer from algorithm bias (more on this in Chapter 2).

▶▶▶▶ Broadly, you can think of an algorithm as a sequence of steps in a process. To introduce the concept to students, ask them about algorithms that they might use every day: their routines for getting ready in the morning or how they prepare a bowl of cereal. What are the steps in the process? Does the order of the steps matter? A fun (but potentially messy) demonstration is to follow their instructions *exactly*. If the steps they tell you are "get a bowl, then put the cereal in the bowl," try to put the whole unopened box in the bowl. If the instruction is "empty the cereal into the bowl," pour it all in. Or, change the order of the instructions so that "open the milk, then pour it on the cereal" comes first and see what happens. Once you clean up, you can dive into a conversation with your students about what went wrong, the importance of detailed instructions in a specific order, and in the case of computers, where (and why) a program might have an error in its code or algorithm.

What Is Machine Learning?

Machine learning (ML) is a component of artificial intelligence in which computer systems enhance their proficiency in tasks by analyzing data and patterns (**Figure 1.1**).

Machine learning relies on algorithms that have been trained on data, such as statistical models. These specialized algorithms then respond to this data, seek patterns in it, and learn from it so they can better analyze new, similar information. As an AI program's knowledge base grows, it will continue to improve on past iterations (as it has been programmed to do), which, in turn, will expand the realm of possibilities for what it can do.

FIGURE 1.1
Infographic showing the components of machine learning

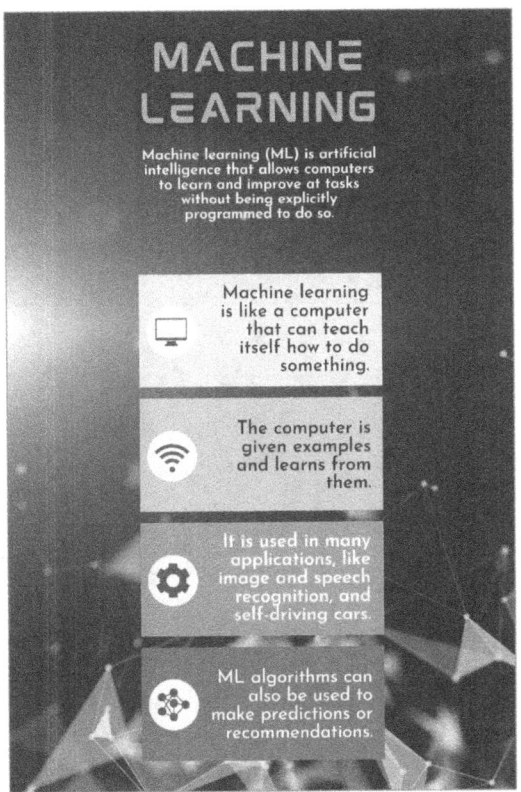

In the context of education, machine learning can analyze student data to recognize patterns and make predictions, making it easier for teachers to act faster to support student learning. Teachers can then use the predictions to tailor learning materials and pace, ensuring individualized instruction for all students. Machine learning can help with early intervention by identifying students at risk of falling behind through predictive analytics, enabling timely intervention and support. Educators can use AI-powered platforms to offer customized content, quizzes, and exercises that meet each student's needs at the time they need it. In addition, AI can automate grading and feedback, which saves time for teachers and provides data-driven insights to help educators identify trends, assess curriculum efficacy, and inform and better target instructional methods.

What Is Natural Language Processing (NLP)?

Natural language processing (NLP) is a component of AI that focuses on the interaction that occurs between computers and human language. With NLP algorithms, computers are able to understand the meaning and structure of human language, analyze text and speech, generate human language, and respond to input via natural-sounding text or audibly. These algorithms act as the bridge between human language and computer code. As with machine learning, NLP systems store and analyze all information (words, sentences, the text of books, and so on) that is loaded into them, and then use this data to find patterns and then generate communication in return.

You're probably interacting with NLP every single day because of all the places it is found. Whether you're asking a question of Amazon's Alexa or another virtual assistant, listening to turn-by-turn directions from Siri as you drive, or answering automated screening questions before speaking to a live customer service representative, you're interacting with NLP. As a means for customers to receive assistance with reduced wait time, many businesses—airlines, banks, credit card companies, hotels, pharmacies, utility companies, and more—use chatbots. *Chatbots* use NLP to engage users in what feels like a human conversation. NLP enables chatbots to understand questions from humans and then generate responses (in text or speech) that mimic a human conversation. They can understand the context of conversations and provide answers within seconds. For example, we can engage in what feels like a real conversation with a chatbot or virtual assistant to manage an account, receive tech support, and even learn a language. Powered by NLP, translation services like Google Translate can automatically translate text or speech from one language to another, which promotes accessibility as it becomes easier for people to communicate and access information. ChatGPT is probably one of the most high-profile and advanced chatbots at this writing. Almost instantly, it accesses information from massive data sets, sorts and processes it, and then compiles a response—even translating that answer into various languages, if necessary. (We'll talk more about how ChatGPT works and its other capabilities in a moment.)

▶▶▶▶ There are endless ways to use this technology to assist with tasks in the world of work and in education. NLP can be used to correct spelling and grammar in documents, for example; or students could write documents by speaking to their computer via speech-to-text functions. NLP can also respond to human language and react based on the information that it receives, as well as evaluate speech based on context and intonation, and then respond. Think about the opportunities for virtual tutors, assistance with building interpersonal skills, developing language skills, practicing for a quiz, preparing for an interview, or simply making materials more accessible to all students. Challenge your students to think of more examples. How have they used NLP functionalities in their everyday lives? How have you used them to your benefit in your work?

What Are Neural Networks?

Building on the complex algorithms of machine learning and NLP, *neural networks* are computational models inspired by the human brain's interconnected neurons. They process information through layers of interconnected nodes, learning patterns from data sets. In education, neural networks are used to enhance tasks like language processing, image recognition, and adaptive learning systems to support students' individual needs. I often tell my students that neural networks function like their brains, sorting and processing information faster than they ever could.

▶▶▶▶ To demonstrate how a neural network functions, you can have your students try Quick, Draw! from Google (**quickdraw.withgoogle.com**). With it, students help a neural network learn to recognize drawings by sketching provided words. The process is similar to playing Pictionary with a computer. While you draw, the neural network tries to guess the object in real time before the twenty-second time limit expires. The neural network refines its guesses by eliminating possibilities based on the shape or design you are using. If you draw a square shape, for example, it eliminates any object that does not match the shape of a square from its guess. To help students understand this process, choose four objects and ask students to identify which object is different and why. This is how the neural network functions in simpler terms.

What Are Generative AI and ChatGPT?

As I mentioned earlier, ChatGPT is one of the most well-known chatbots. It is also an example of a *large language model* (*LLM*), a generative AI tool that is built upon deep learning and neural networks, trained on massive amounts of data, and capable of understanding human language and generating new content. *Generative AI tools* can understand and respond to prompts to complete endless types of tasks and create a variety of content such as images, music, text, videos, and more. (Chapter 4 focuses on generative AI and ideas for its uses.)

Developed by OpenAI, ChatGPT is an upgrade from GPT-3 (Generative Pre-Trained Transformer 3), a trained language model that uses deep learning and can simulate human conversation. Through the use of a *prompt* (think of this like a writing prompt you'd give your students), you can ask it anything ranging from providing a description of something with examples to creating a lesson plan or rubric for your class to generating project ideas to providing relevant definitions or detailed descriptions—and so much more.

Within seconds, ChatGPT analyzes the prompt you entered and generates a response by using algorithms and sorting through the massive data that it can access. The use of deep learning algorithms enables it to understand the context and meaning of the prompt, which it then uses to create its response in a conversational manner. ChatGPT can also learn from your interactions with it to adapt and improve its responses. Does this mean that the answer is always perfect and exactly what you're looking for? Not necessarily. Sometimes you have to tweak it or ask it to regenerate a response, which is why we need to focus on prompt engineering (Chapter 4 offers ideas to help you craft effective prompts). It sounds great because of all of the ways that you can use ChatGPT to save time, gather resources, analyze text, and more (Chapter 3 elaborates with even more benefits); however, generative AI tools like ChatGPT bring with them concerns surrounding ethical use, information accuracy, and academic integrity (more on this in Chapter 2). The technology has been advancing rapidly, especially with the capabilities of GPT-4 Turbo, which has additional generative capabilities and access to more current data.

ChatGPT is not the only generative AI tool available. As a class, generative AI (or GenAI as it is often called) tools have been trained on massive amounts of data to recognize patterns and relationships among words, images, sounds, and even code. They can create new content, learn patterns from existing data, and then use it to generate new and unique output, such as text for news articles, blog posts, and even creative writing; images in the style of photographs, paintings, and cartoons; realistic, human-sounding voices for audiobooks, music, and podcasts; and video for movies, TV shows, and ads. Its uses in the world and in education are increasing rapidly, as you'll learn in Chapter 4, which dives deeper into working with ChatGPT, DALL•E, and other GenAI tools.

By Andrew Easton, speaker, author, consultant, and Digital Learning Coordinator for Nebraska's Educational Service Unit Coordinating Council

Generative artificial intelligence has revolutionized education by providing a variety of benefits for enhancing teaching and learning. It significantly assists educators in making personalized learning a realistic goal for all students in our classrooms. In the field of education, time is such a precious and limited resource, and AI tools have significantly impacted the efficiency of both teachers and students when it comes to tailoring lessons to the individual needs of learners. Many tasks that educators must complete each day are time-consuming. By using generative AI, they can get back some of that time and spend it working more closely with students instead.

For example, generative AI chatbots excel at rephrasing texts to make accommodations for things like text complexity, sentence structures, Lexile levels, and more. These capabilities are tremendously helpful for differentiation and promoting more accessibility in the classroom. Generative AI text-to-video tools can transfer learning to a different modality, one with visuals that might present fewer barriers for those still growing in their ability to read to learn. The inverse is true as well. AI tools can create a text transcript of any video content, and they can do so in virtually any language. From there, they can extract the main ideas and key vocabulary or even create comprehension questions for learners to consider while reading (or viewing) the information. Generative AI chatbots can also be prompted to create a simulation or take on the persona or role of, say, a historical figure, academic tutor, or debate opponent. This practice empowers each student to learn through dialogue that honors their individual questions, makes space for their own claims, and engages them in a much richer and deeper learning experience. These experiences also foster creativity and critical thinking skills in students by helping develop an understanding of how GenAI can be used to enhance their understanding of the content and engage them more in a unique learning experience.

In short, generative artificial intelligence is driving the kind of transformative change that education has always aspired to but has been unable to live out due to limited time, resources, and support.

AI in Our Lives

▶▶▶▶ A good way to learn about any emerging technology is to make time for discussion. Here are a few guiding questions to help you start conversations about AI with your students:

✦ What do you know?

✦ What do you want to know?

+ What concerns do you have?

+ What are some things that are seen as positives about the technology, and where do we go from here?

When I bring AI to the students in my classroom, I first define some terms, then share some examples of its use before diving into the tools and exploring the technology's capabilities and limitations (yes, the same approach I'm following in this book). Now that you understand some of the vocabulary of AI, let's look at some areas where we are already interacting with and benefiting from machine learning and AI. (We will dig deeper into some of these in Chapters 4 and 5.)

+ **Communication:** Artificial intelligence is capable of analyzing multiple forms of communication and streamlining some functionalities. Email spam filters, for example, reduce the amount of spam that appears in your inbox by using machine-learning algorithms to analyze incoming mail for specific words and patterns. As spam senders (real or automated) use more caution to avoid previously flagged words, your email provider's filters adapt to recognize new suspicious patterns, thus learning and improving over time.

+ **Education:** In the last five years, the number of resources available to teachers and students has grown tremendously: tools for assisting with creating citations, plagiarism checkers, game-based learning tools, spelling and grammar checkers, text auto-completion features, and more. Each of these runs on algorithms and can be a great help to students. While a grammar checker like Grammarly can provide support, however, students still need to rely on their own skills. Likewise, think about all the information you can access within less than a second of conducting a Google search—all possible through AI. To help students navigate this sometimes overwhelming volume, we need to have guidelines in place for both students and educators. Sharing these with families as well will help support students in their learning at home.

+ **Online shopping:** Making purchases has changed so much because of AI. Amazon and other shopping sites now routinely suggest items that you may be interested in by analyzing your prior searches, your order history, and similar shopping patterns of other people. (And don't forget the pervasive ads that appear once you've searched for a brand, product, or service.) AI also helps to protect consumers against fraud. Credit card companies and banks employ systems that send alerts immediately upon attempted transactions that do not fit a consumer's purchasing patterns or that occur outside that person's typical geographical location.

- **Social networking:** AI is built into many social networking sites. For example, when you share a photo on Facebook, AI can detect faces in the image and suggest names of the people as tags. The facial recognition improves over time as you frequently tag the same person. This is an example of *deep learning*, a subset of machine learning, and only one of Facebook's AI-based features designed to generate more personalized and interactive user experiences (Abdulkader et al., 2016). Other social media sites, such as X (formerly Twitter), use AI to suggest accounts to follow and chats to join, and can also generate news feeds based on an analysis of user input and data. Google personalizes your experience through cards that use AI to make personal recommendations based on your search history. It populates your feed with stories that may interest you based on places you've visited, restaurants you've eaten in, or articles you've read. When you provide feedback, using a thumbs-up or thumbs-down, it learns and improves the results that it provides you.

- **Travel:** Ride-share services like Uber and Lyft use machine learning to predict rider demand and to calculate your driver's estimated arrival time. When you use the app, it scans for available drivers, connects you with one, shares your exact location with them, and estimates your arrival time at your destination. This all happens almost instantly, thanks to AI technology processing information related to traffic, distances, times, and availability. In the airline industry, autopilot can be considered a type of AI, and its use accounts for all but seven minutes of the average commercial flight (Julien, 2019).

Why Bring AI Into the Classroom?

We are interacting with AI every day, and our students need to understand what it is. More than that, they need to know how it works, the impact that it has on our lives, and what it might mean for the future of work and education. With the right resources, we can create learning opportunities that will spark student curiosity and help them build skills in these emerging technologies. David Touretzky at Carnegie Mellon University leads the AI4K12 organization, which provides many resources for learning about AI. One of the most helpful that I refer to is their Five Big Ideas in Artificial Intelligence poster (**Figure 1.2**). Understanding each of these Big Ideas helps students better process exactly what AI does and its impact.

FIGURE 1.2
AI4K12's Five Big Ideas
in AI. You can down-
load a detailed poster
of the ideas from
ai4k12.org.

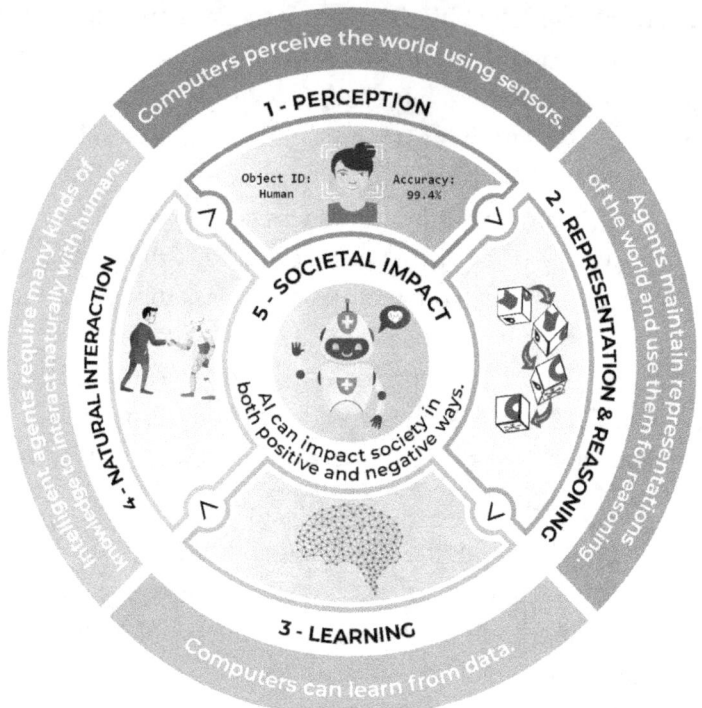

While it is important that everyone in the school is involved in the learning process, teachers are "considered among the most crucial stakeholders in AI-based teaching" (Celik, 2023). And it is important to get more comfortable teaching about AI so we can support students along the way. By helping our students understand AI, we can help them shift from being consumers of information to becoming the creators and innovators. "Innovation in education is not just a matter of putting more technology into more classrooms; it is about changing approaches to teaching so that students acquire the skills they need to be successful and reach their academic goals and AI can support these goals" (Crompton & Burke, 2022, p. 113).

As educators, having access to something that helps us sort through student data in a short period of time—thus freeing up time to interact with students one on one—is beneficial for teachers and our students. Think about the amount of time that it takes to look over student work, grade assessments, and provide feedback. All of this is fundamentally important for student learning, and being able to save valuable time through the use of technology means we can instead spend that time with our students. Using AI to instantly access resources that offer more personalized learning for students in real time is where I think the true benefits of AI in education lie.

✨Activity: Reflect On AI in Your Life

From fitness trackers to cameras to navigation aids, AI is behind so many things we take for granted these days that we often don't realize we're interacting with it. Start a conversation (in your classroom or with your peers) to become more aware of AI's many uses in everyday life. This chapter lists many examples; what are some others that you can think of? How often do you rely on these services? What did you do before these capabilities existed? What are their positives and negatives?

Here is a sampling of more questions for you and your students to reflect on:

+ How often do you (or family members) rely on virtual assistants to catch up on the latest news, ask a question, make a purchase, or set personal reminders?

+ Do you (or your family) have smart home devices?

+ Do you unlock your phone using facial recognition (or do you know any adults who do)?

+ Do you (or family members) place orders through Amazon or another online service that can automate?

+ How do these capabilities enhance or improve the task?

Consider how frequently these technologies are used, their benefits, and their negative effects. All of these are convenient and can save us time, but we need to be conscious of the potential negatives that come with them too. By automating tasks, AI technologies can help us be more efficient or eliminate the need for a human to complete the task—is this a positive (we can turn our attention to other pursuits) or a negative (AI may take away jobs from people)?

The big issue is not *if* AI will change the world, but how much has it *already* changed the world. Create a space to have conversations with your students, and keep learning and exploring together. In Chapter 2, we'll tackle some important privacy and ethical issues surrounding AI to help you expand the conversation even further.

Where to Learn More

There are many resources available to help you develop a greater understanding of AI. For example, Getting Smart's *AI in Education* whitepaper offers background information, talking points to use with your students, policy suggestions, case studies, and much more. The book *Artificial Intelligence in Education* by Wayne Holmes, Maya Bialik, and Charles Fadel is a thorough and informative read to understand the full history of artificial intelligence, while Nishant Sirohi's article "Artificial Intelligence: An Explainer for Beginners" is a good overview of key AI issues. You can find additional resource suggestions to further your understanding in Appendix B or by scanning the QR code.

tinyurl.com/ykt7c8z9

Key Takeaways

In this chapter, we focused on key terms (**Figure 1.3**), the importance of educators learning how AI works, and where we see this technology in our everyday lives. With a solid foundation, we can better support our students in understanding this quickly evolving topic.

As educators, we need to develop an understanding of emerging technologies so that we are prepared to share learning experiences, collaborate, and co-learn with students. (*ISTE Standards 2.1.c Learner, 2.2.c Leader, 2.4.b Collaborator*)

We need to stay current with research and mentor students in the ethical and responsible use of AI tools. (*ISTE Standards 2.1.c Learner, 2.2.c Leader, 2.3.c Citizen*)

With our help, students will then grow to understand emerging AI technologies and how they can use these tools to explore real-world issues and problems. (*ISTE Standards 1.1.d Empowered Learner, 1.3.d Knowledge Constructor, 1.4.d Innovative Designer, 1.5.d Computational Thinker*)

FIGURE 1.3

A visual review of the key terms of artificial intelligence

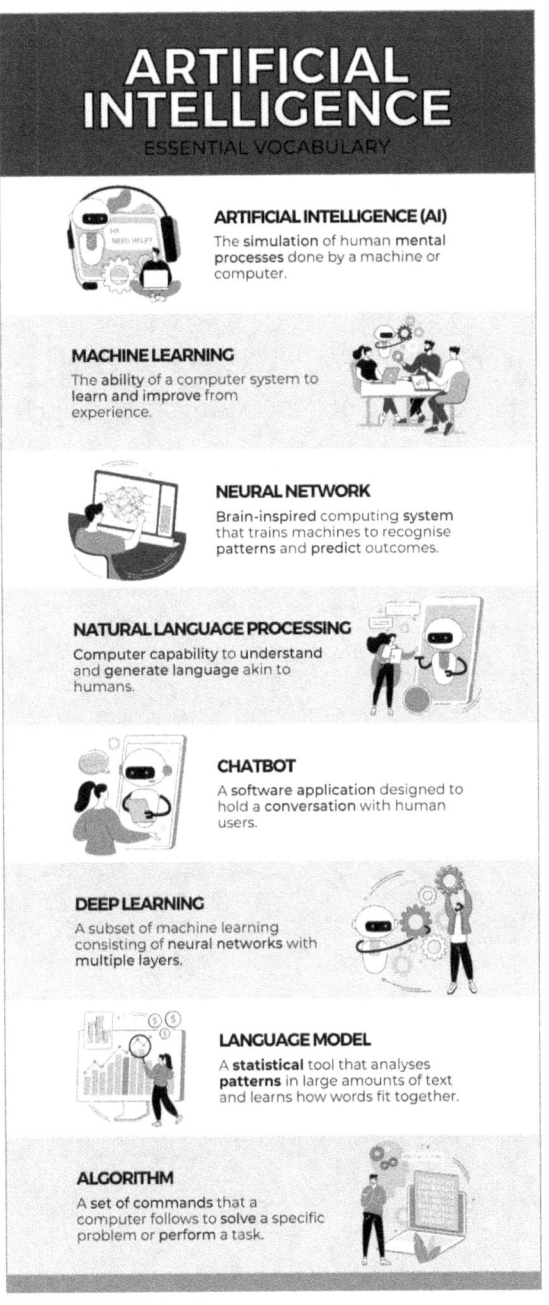

Questions for Reflection and Discussion

Before you dive into the next chapter, take a moment to reflect on what you've learned in this one.

✦ What concerns do you have when it comes to AI?

✦ What are some areas where you believe that AI will help you in your classroom or school?

✦ As an educator, why do you think it is important to learn about AI?

✦ How do you plan to start teaching about or using AI in your classroom?

Share your ideas with me on X (formerly Twitter) @Rdene915 or post a message on LinkedIn.

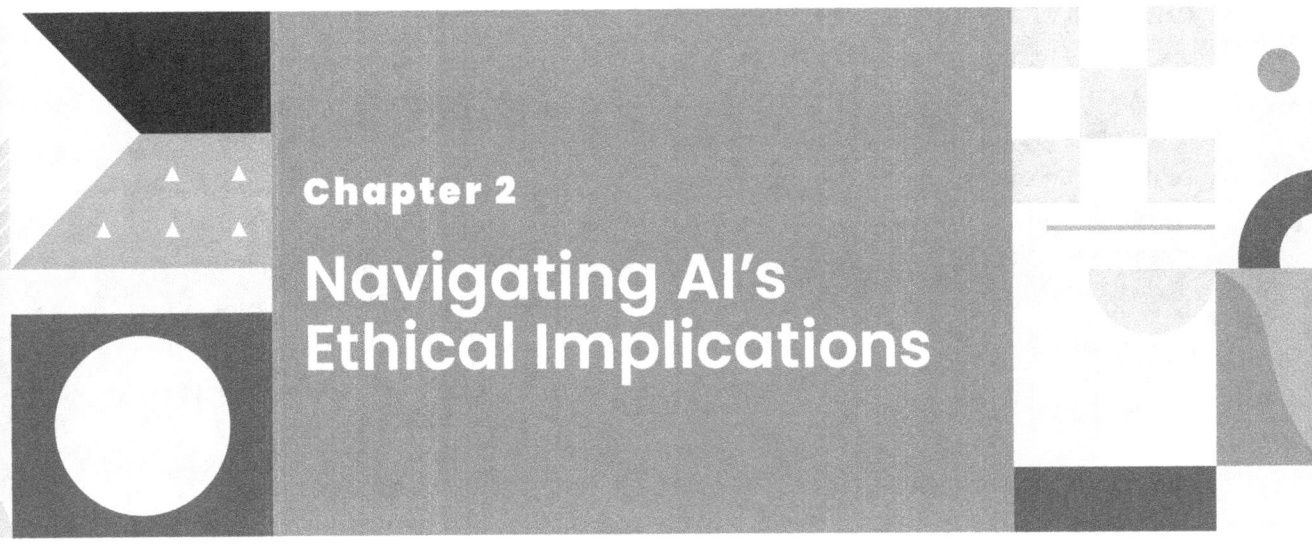

Chapter 2

Navigating AI's Ethical Implications

The content of this chapter aligns with the following standards and indicators:

ISTE Student Standards

1.2.a, 1.2.d Digital Citizen

ISTE Educator Standards

2.2.a, 2.2.b, 2.2.c Leader

2.3.c Citizen

ISTE Education Leader Standards

3.1.d Equity and Citizenship Advocate

3.3.d Empowering Leader

3.4.c Systems Designer

CHAPTER 1 FOCUSED on the positives that come with the use of AI; however, its use also comes with potential risks and ethical concerns. As educators, we have a responsibility to make sure that our students understand how to minimize the impact of those risks while reaping the benefits that AI-powered technologies offer. For example, we have an essential role in teaching students about the ethical implications of biases that can emerge in AI algorithms. Teachers, administrators, and IT staff must work together to research and vet the tools adopted by their school for responsible use of AI and to ensure that the ways the tools are being used are beneficial, not detrimental, to our students or society. In this chapter, we'll explore the ethical implications of AI and specifically AI in the classroom, including biases and fairness, accountability challenges, and the impact on privacy and security, so that you can better prepare your students.

We'll also discuss the importance of having ongoing conversations surrounding these issues, both with your fellow educators about specific school policies and with students in your classroom. To address challenges and concerns that may be present now or that may arise as AI technology continues to evolve, schools need to develop policies and guidelines for educators and then share these with families to help everyone better understand the ethical considerations related to AI. In our classrooms, educators need to find ways to make learning about ethics and having conversations part of the work that we do to help our students be well-prepared for their future.

In my own classroom, students initially brought up ethical considerations around AI. During one of my early units with my eighth graders, a lesson about facial recognition led to a conversation about bias, misidentification, and their impact. We talked about bias in other areas too, such as self-driving cars and how they are programmed. When creating the underlying algorithms, humans had to make the decisions of how the self-driving car would adjust to different situations, such as pedestrians crossing or other traffic-related issues. Students were very engaged in these discussions, and with each passing lesson, they had more questions. They wanted to explore more. Since those days of early 2018, national and international AI-focused organizations have formed, and several provide free resources, lessons, and more to help educators and students explore the ethics of AI. (You'll learn more about these later in the chapter.) My students also expressed that they felt as though ethics was a topic that should be discussed more in all of their classes. They were right! Such discussions help students develop the skills to make ethical decisions throughout their lives and to consider others' perspectives.

Why Teaching AI Ethics Matters

According to Akgun and Greenhow (2022), there are several risks that come with the integration of AI algorithms into the educational system in grades K through 12. Those risks include "a) perpetuating existing systemic bias and discrimination, b) perpetuating unfairness for students from mostly disadvantaged and marginalized groups, and c) amplifying racism, sexism, xenophobia, and other forms of injustice and inequity" (Akgun & Greenhow, 2022). These are serious concerns, and "the famous scientist, Stephen Hawking, pointed out that weighing these risks is vital for the future of humanity. Therefore, it is critical to take action toward addressing them" (Akgun & Greenhow, 2022).

Making sure that discussions about ethics become part of the conversations in your school is a key action that will help the school community stay aware of areas of concern and work together to find solutions. As this technology continues to evolve, new challenges and concerns will arise. We need to be prepared to discuss them and to continue to reflect on how AI is impacting or might impact our work and our world. We educators have a responsibility to continue learning about AI and the negative potential outcomes of using it in our schools, and to then transfer our knowledge to our students. Students and teachers both need a variety of opportunities to learn about AI with access to resources and a curriculum focused on ethics. Teachers need professional development opportunities on these topics in their schools, while students need our guidance to build AI literacy skills and develop habits that will enable them to be successful throughout the inevitable changes spawned by AI.

So How Do We Get Started?

Knowing that we need to understand the ethical implications of AI and knowing how best to teach students about them are two different things. So, how do you start? Begin by modeling ethical use of AI tools and encouraging conversations in your classroom. No matter your grade level or content area, you can integrate conversations about ethics into your classroom to build responsible digital citizens. Engaging students in meaningful and rich discussions will help them learn to express their opinions, as well as develop their social awareness, empathy, and tolerance of diverse perspectives. They must learn how to protect themselves and to advocate for others when it comes to the impact of this technology.

But having those conversations is not always easy. Maybe you feel you don't have enough experience or knowledge in the area to guide students. Perhaps you don't know where to start and lack resources to help you. Depending on the topic, in trying to cover everything that falls under the umbrella of AI ethics, you may run up on the rocks of difficult or uncomfortable conversations.

Educating yourself on the ethical implications of using AI tools and technology can help overcome these challenges. By gaining a good understanding of the issues and areas to focus on, you will be better able to provide learning opportunities for students so that they can then learn about ethics and put what they learn into practice. In the following sections, we'll discuss some of the most serious ethical focus points to help you get ready for your own discussions with students.

Areas of Ethical Concern

AI use is growing exponentially—not just in education, but everywhere—and the programming and resources that power it also drive the ethical concerns around its use. For example, algorithms may have built-in biases that discriminate against certain populations, such as minorities or underrepresented groups. Being aware of this will help you avoid perpetuating bias. We also need to be mindful of safeguarding information to ensure that the privacy of individuals is not impacted negatively as a result of AI. We need to be able to distinguish between real information and misinformation, such as through the use of AI-generated "fake news" or deep fakes designed to commit fraudulent activities or sow confusion and dissent. Massive amounts of resources are required for AI technology as well, which can negatively impact the environment. So we need to understand the risk-benefit of this technology and be able to have conversations with the right stakeholders so that we can make the best choices moving forward. Let's look more closely at each of these ethical concerns, as well as resources and activities you can use to help students understand them.

Bias in AI

Bias is a human trait, and human programmers creating and training AI algorithms can inadvertently infuse their biases into those programs. If an AI system is trained on data that is biased toward a certain group, for example, it could then make decisions favoring that group at the expense of others. Likewise, training data that is incomplete can create unexpected and negative results.

Consider the free version of ChatGPT from OpenAI, for example. Originally, it was trained with information that existed on the web prior to January of 2022. In other words, it didn't know about anything that has happened since December of 2021. Nor do *we* know who created the information developers used to train ChatGPT, whether it's accurate, and if any of it demonstrates bias (either by inclusion or omission). When you type a prompt for ChatGPT, therefore, the answer it generates may be useful or it may potentially be biased, inappropriate, or just plain wrong. Because ChatGPT is a *large language model (LLM)*, it sorts through all the data sets it learned and uses that information to generate a response—but without a human component to adjust its language use or to check whether it exhibits bias. That bias cannot be attributed to any specific person (certainly not the one who typed the prompt). ChatGPT simply pulled in the information that it was programmed with; the bias was already there. In November of 2023, OpenAI released ChatGPT Plus, an upgraded, paid version based on GPT-4 that includes more recent data sets, the ability to explore custom-trained chatbots and upload documents and images, and even a make-your-own bot feature—but it still has the potential for bias.

To minimize bias in AI algorithms, developers need to have safeguards in place to ensure that the training data they use is diverse and representative of all groups. They need to use a data set that was mindfully created and reviewed to check for any potential issues. When an algorithm trains on data that AI pulls in from endless online resources, biased or unverified information may be included, and then the algorithm will produce biased or inaccurate results or gaps in the knowledge of the information that is shared. Remember the old programmer's adage: garbage in, garbage out.

Regular monitoring and testing of the algorithms is essential to help identify and address any biases or inaccuracies that may arise. Being able to critically analyze the information that AI tools produce is key.

Likewise, as users, we need to carefully evaluate the practices and tools that we are using in our classrooms and monitor them for any signs of potential bias. Schools should review classroom practices to make sure that AI is being used in a responsible and ethical way. They should also conduct ongoing audits of digital tools to make sure they are in compliance with such data privacy regulations as COPPA (Children's Online Privacy and Protection Act) and FERPA (Family Educational Rights and Privacy Act) and also evaluate what data is being collected and how it may be shared with third parties. It is important to have an ongoing system of review in place to ensure the ethical, responsible, and safe use of these tools. ChatGPT is not the only AI system to keep an eye on, either. Other LLMs, such as Google Gemini, Microsoft Bing, and Claude 3, also need to be monitored to see if bias is present in the responses and how the results improve over time. As these tools evolve, audits should be revisited to ensure that ethical practices are being followed.

AI Bias and Education

Bias in AI algorithms can have a negative impact in education. It can perpetuate discrimination and inequity among students. If a tool was programmed or trained on data that focused more on a certain population or demographic, using it can result in inequities in the learning experiences for students. The impact of this then could lead to unfair treatment of students and negatively impact their academic progress.

How can we potentially mitigate the bias? In our classrooms, we can build awareness of the potential for bias and how it occurs. We need to engage in conversations about bias with our students, some of whom may become programmers later in life.

Start Conversations with Students

Teaching about bias in AI involves highlighting how biases can be unintentionally embedded in algorithms due to biased training data or biased design decisions. You can engage students in critical discussions on the real-world consequences of biased AI, such as perpetuating stereotypes or discrimination. By your emphasizing the social impact of biased AI, students can develop a deeper understanding of the ethical responsibilities involved in AI development and implementation.

With a variety of learning activities, you can empower students to think critically about the biases that exist in data and algorithms and push students to think about how to handle these issues. With so many concerns about improper use or reliance on AI, there are opportunities to build the essential skills that students need. By teaching students to analyze different AI systems, identify potential biases, and discuss them with classmates, you can help cultivate a generation of AI users who are mindful of the ethical considerations related to AI. Students will be better equipped to actively address bias in AI systems and be open to conversations about bias. We have a responsibility to our students to bring opportunities to them so we can foster a greater understanding of the issues related to ethics and how to apply that thinking to real-world applications. The "Resources for Teaching Ethics and AI" and "Activities: Addressing Ethical Dilemmas" sections later in this chapter offer some ideas on how to get started.

EDUCATOR'S PERSPECTIVE: TEACHING ETHICS

By Dr. Torrey Trust and Robert W. Maloy, University of Massachusetts Amherst, Massachusetts (adapted from "Learning about Civics and Government: The Ethics of AI in Political Campaigns")

Utilizing Kwane Anthony Appiah's "The Ethicist" column in the New York Times Magazine as the starting point for instructional ideas, we envision giving elementary, middle, and high school students ongoing opportunities to develop their own ethical responses to authentic questions and issues they are facing in their lives, schools, and communities—especially those related to the use of GenAI tools and large language models (LLMs)—as a means of helping them develop their civic engagement skills and knowledge. Ideally, students engage in discussions about how they and others should act in the different situations and settings of everyday life. By stating their views and restating and understanding the views of others, students will become more socially conscious and civically engaged as members of our diverse society.

For example, following the model of "The Ethicist," students could be asked: Is it ethical to use GenAI tools to craft political campaign materials and media? To begin this activity, students could be encouraged to use the Teacher and Student Guide to Analyzing AI Writing Tools (see Appendix B) to critically investigate popular GenAI tools, including ChatGPT, Google Gemini, Stable Diffusion, and DALL·E. The guide consists of a set of critical media literacy questions that students and teachers, collaboratively or individually, can ask as they investigate the design, production, language, and distribution of AI tools. Throughout the activity, students could focus on questions such as:

- What data was used to train this tool?

- What biases are represented in the data?

- What privacy protections are in place for users' data?

Through this type of critical investigation, students might uncover that GenAI tools are trained on data that has embedded biases and consider what that might mean, in this case, for political campaigns.

Intellectual Property and Academic Integrity

Teaching about plagiarism and academic integrity has long been important for all classrooms, and the rise of AI adds a new twist. Students already had easy access to vast amounts of information on the internet, and now large language models like ChatGPT make finding and repurposing that information even easier, increasing the opportunity for the misuse of information. These tools are changing the way humans create, consume, and evaluate content; for instance, financial reports, sports news, and legal briefs are increasingly computer drafted.

AI AND COPYRIGHTS CONVERSATION STARTER

In December of 2023, the *New York Times* filed a lawsuit against OpenAI, the developer of ChatGPT, and Microsoft, the developer of Copilot, alleging copyright infringement and that the companies had copied and used "millions" of the newspaper's articles to train their large language models (Roth, 2023). The suit goes on to claim that OpenAI's and Microsoft's tools "can generate output that recites *Times* content verbatim, closely summarizes it, and mimics its expressive style," which "'undermine[s] and damage[s]' the *Times*' relationship with readers" (Roth, 2023). The *Times* goes on to assert that "these AI models 'threaten high-quality journalism' by hurting the ability of news outlets to protect and monetize content" (Roth, 2023). Meanwhile, Open AI and Microsoft see the matter differently, claiming that "the *Times*' works are considered 'fair use,' which gives them the ability to use copyrighted material for a 'transformative purpose'" (Duffy & Goldman, 2023).

▶▶▶▶ What do your students think? Does AI-generated content threaten traditional journalism? Is repurposing content without identifying its source "fair use"? Use the case to start a conversation about the importance of copyrights and giving credit to the source. Ask students to create a list of pros and cons of using AI-generated content, and give them time to brainstorm ideas and then engage in an open discussion to further explore their ideas.

We need to engage students in conversations about copyrights and the importance of properly citing resources that they use in reports, projects, and more. When using AI tools, students are gathering information from the data sets the tools were trained on but without any details or guidance on that information's original source or creator. Therefore, we have to guide students on proper use and citation of sources.

At the same time, we also must help students understand that while using AI can help them build skills, using these tools isn't a replacement for learning those skills. If they use AI tools to complete an assignment or a project, they still must demonstrate that they have developed the skills the assignment was designed to help them build.

When discussing this and responsible use of AI with students, I use an analogy: They can pretend they've learned to play a saxophone, pressing its keys in convincing fashion in time to recorded music—maybe adding some puffed cheeks and rhythmic swaying for flair—but what happens when they're asked to play that same song alone in front of a crowd without the recording? They won't be able to do it because they've just been mimicking the act of playing the instrument, not learning the skill. The same is true of relying too heavily on AI tools to complete assignments. In my language class, students relying on translation tools may be able to work through the material; however, when asked to engage in a conversation in class or to perform a certain task in the target language, they will less likely be able to do so.

"But how," educators often ask, "can I tell when a student has used AI to 'write' an assignment?" You can tell because, like me, you know your students, you've built relationships with them, and you've seen them build their skills over time. For example, many of the AI-powered tools we use have Microsoft's Immersive Reader built in, which means students can use it to translate for them and submit the tool's results as their own work. Will they be discovered? Yes, especially when the writing contains language content that I've not yet covered in their course level! Students all have their own signature style of expressing thoughts whether verbally or in writing that AI can't imitate. When you have an understanding of where your students are in the learning process and the type of work that they might produce, you can better spot the fake. Getting to know our students and openly having discussions with them is a critical part of learning about and bringing AI into the classroom.

More importantly, you can guide students to use AI responsibly and appropriately while they focus on developing their own skills. You help them understand why such academic integrity is important. If they push back, explain that you need to know what they have *learned*, not what they have copied from a website and not that they're skillful at having someone or something else create results for them.

Remember, ChatGPT is simply a tool that students can use to help them learn and understand. Just like with other tools from printed encyclopedias to Google searches, the key is understanding when and how to use it in a way that is appropriate, ethical, and responsible. We have to model for our students the right ways to use this technology, share with them what we see as the benefits, and take time to explore together to identify concerns or potential negatives of using ChatGPT. For example, its answers may contain "copied content, wrong replies and improper referencing (or no referencing at all)" (Gill et al., 2024, p. 21). To help your students demonstrate genuine learning while benefiting from AI assistance, here are a few reminders you can give them:

✦ Always give credit to the source. If AI was used, how was it used? Follow the APA or MLA guidelines for citing ChatGPT, for example. See more via the Grammarly site (**grammarly.com/blog/ai-citations-mla**).

- Rely on your own thoughts and knowledge base first. Use AI tools as a reference or a means of enhancing the work you are doing.

- Remember to check the accuracy of information.

EDUCATOR'S PERSPECTIVE: LEARNING FROM CHEATING WITH AI

By Nicole Biscotti, Spanish teacher and author, Southern California

A lot of educators are wary of AI in the classroom because they are concerned about cheating. In reality, it's more important for educators to understand *why* kids cheat than to try to create a cheating-proof classroom by resisting technology. The reasons that kids cheat provide insight that we can use to provide more effective support for our students. Often the support needed is related to executive functions, connection to the content, pacing issues, or clearer expectations. We have an opportunity to partner with students rather than fight a never-ending battle to stop the advancement of technology.

Teachers can easily detect cheating either by the use of technology or simply by AI's flat tone and general lack of depth. Encouraging students to identify places where more depth, details, perspective, or evidence would enhance an AI-generated writing piece is a powerful and prac-tical lesson. AI offers a plethora of executive functioning supports such as the ability to create a schedule, a summary, an outline; to provide definitions and synonyms; and so on. Best of all, students can use the accessibility of AI to become more independent learners who are aware of the type of support they need.

By understanding how students use AI tools, we can determine how better to help them use these tools while also infusing their own voice and learning progress into their work. By doing this, we can provide the best support for their growth.

Protecting Students' Data and Privacy

Websites and apps collecting or asking us to input personal information is nothing new, and protecting personally identifiable information (name, address, academic informa-tion, driver's license number, social security number, and the like) has been a pillar of good digital citizenship for years. Now, the aggressive growth and use of AI are raising the stakes. AI-powered systems have the capability to collect, analyze, and store massive amounts of data—not simply the details we *choose* to provide when signing up for an account somewhere, but also data regarding our shopping habits, Google searches, social media posts, and more. When you complete online surveys, for example, these programs are able to track your information, process it, and exchange it, in most cases without us even knowing. Exactly what information is being obtained from us, and where is that information then going?

People everywhere are relying on the convenience of technology without considering how much personal data is at risk. We simply put trust in the tools and the platforms that we are using. It's time to take a closer look at the tools we're using in our schools (not to mention in our everyday lives) to ensure that they are in alignment with policies and the specific guidelines created to protect students and their information. For example, federal guidelines, such as COPPA, FERPA, and ADA (Americans with Disabilities Act) are in place to make sure that student privacy is maintained; however, we know that these are not necessarily always complied with. It's important to make sure that we provide students, their families, and educators in our schools with information they need to understand the types of tools that they will be using and how the information may be stored or shared, and give them the choice to opt out of using some of these in order to protect their privacy. The Acceptable Use Policy (AUP) in each school should be reviewed as the technology evolves, as well. It is also important to engage in ongoing review of the tools being used and check their privacy settings to make sure that we are protecting our students and educators.

Providing another tool to help manage the risks of AI, on October 30, 2023, U.S. President Biden released an Executive Order on "safe, secure, and trustworthy artificial intelligence" (The White House, 2023). The goals of the Executive Order are to set standards for AI safety and security, to protect privacy, while also promoting innovation. It provides guidelines for companies to follow that require they share safety test results and other critical information with the U.S. government. It directs that standards must be set to ensure safety, security, and protection from fraudulent actions or invasions of privacy. The Order also focuses on advancing equity and civil rights by addressing "algorithmic discrimination through training, technical assistance, and coordination between the Department of Justice and Federal civil rights offices on best practices for investigating and prosecuting civil rights violations related to AI" (The White House, 2023).

Although we have guidelines and standards in place that help protect personal data (and the promise of more in the future), there is no guarantee that tool developers and online companies are in compliance with them. Always check a website to see exactly how it uses any information that it obtains and any disclaimers that are provided. Sometimes a site's Frequently Asked Questions (FAQs) page will explain policies regarding the use of data. Will user-provided data be used only by the website itself, or will it be shared with other third parties or other interconnected platforms? It's important to understand how you or your students' private and sensitive information may be shared and what steps you can take to ensure everyone's privacy is protected and not compromised. Think of the steps such as reviewing privacy settings, log-in procedures, and checking for resources that describe the types of information being collected.

When logging in, submitting your information on a site, or making a purchase, you may have to check a box to prove you're not a robot or to complete a CAPTCHA (Completed Automated Public Turing test to tell Computers and Humans Apart) test. These are in place to help protect personal information and provide you with the security of knowing that your information is not being misused by a bot or compromised. It has been set to prove that a human and not a robot is entering the information. These tests have become more complex as technology, especially AI, has evolved. As a result, there is research being done to determine whether these tests are still effective, especially with the rise of bots that can perform the same tasks and even some CAPTCHA codes faster than humans (Lagatta, 2023).

✦ Activity: Understanding Data Collection and Privacy

To help students understand the importance of protecting their information as well as the prevalence of data collection, ask them to investigate a website that might seek information from the user. Depending on the grade level, this activity could be done as a whole class focused on analyzing one website or in groups. In class, break students into groups, give each one a category (privacy settings, social media accounts, pop-up ads), and then provide a list of things for students to look for on their chosen website.

For example, the list could ask them to track the type of information that the website asks the user for or whether the website provides a disclaimer about the accuracy of information, especially if it's a generative AI site. The list should also ask students to find out if and how the site shares user information with third parties. Remind groups that if they are asked for names or other personally identifiable information, they should input made-up names or choose a fictional character, for example. After the groups research their answers, engage the whole class in a discussion about what each group found, the concerns those findings raise, and how these concerns could be addressed. As students share their responses, discuss the types of questions they were asked (such as gender or ethnicity) and consider how those responses could be used without one's permission or to further any potential bias inherent in the AI algorithms powering the data collection.

To culminate the project and demonstrate their understanding, students could even launch a PSA campaign about the importance of safeguarding personal information online, highlighting how websites powered with AI technology may collect, store, and then share your information. Students will learn from this experience, and sharing what they have learned with others is important and makes learning more meaningful and relevant.

Remember: Companies may use our information without our consent. Never use real names, addresses, or other personally identifiable information when testing out generative AI. Substitute the names and locations entered while using a tool, and then make an adjustment once you have left the site in order to protect yourself and the privacy of others.

Facial Recognition

To many people, facial recognition is simply a harmless way to unlock their phone by looking at it. AI-based facial recognition software goes far beyond this convenient feature, however, and raises more privacy issues. We can be surrounded by this technology and potentially not even realize it. Social media networks like Facebook, for example, use facial recognition algorithms to analyze images and detect people. Each time you tag a person in a photo, the AI algorithm learns and stores the name associated with the face, so that the next time you add a photo with that person, the facial recognition improves, eventually enabling the app to automatically tag the person for you in a post. While the practice of tagging friends in photos may seem harmless, it places their privacy at risk and it is sometimes incorrect. Remind students of this and also share with them how to set their privacy settings on the various social media platforms used, depending on their age. Many people may not realize that they have been tagged in an image and are surprised to find their image online. Checking privacy settings is essential, and determining whether you choose to allow people to tag you or not can offer additional protection and greater privacy. The use of facial recognition goes beyond what we post online.

In 2020, for example, Clearview AI, a software company specializing in facial recognition, was embroiled in a controversy regarding privacy laws and the company's practice of gathering images from the internet, including from social media, without the image poster's knowledge or consent. *New York Times* reporter Kashmir Hill first broke the story and exposed how Clearview AI was taking the images and then adding them to a database, initially used by government and law enforcement agencies, who would pay to have access. Clearview had 3 million images at first and now has more than 40 billion (Patel, 2023). The company was determined not to be violating privacy laws, however, because the images were taken from the internet and individuals had placed them on the internet. There were millions of images out there for anyone to use (Patel, 2023). Restrictions on how they can use and profit from the data that they have accumulated have since been placed on Clearview AI (American Civil Liberties Union, 2022). In 2023 several states and even the U.K. sought action from governments to put protection in place to safeguard privacy (Sierra, 2023). As a result, Clearview AI was required to provide an "opt-out" form for residents of certain states to request privacy (American Civil Liberties Union, 2022).

Rite Aid also drew legal fire for using facial recognition for eight years without consent, as a way to "identify shoppers that were previously deemed likely to engage in shoplifting" and creating a database of "persons of interest" that included images and other identifying information (Bhuiyan, 2023). The facial recognition software misidentified thousands of people, in particular female, Black, Asian, and Latinx customers, who were removed from the store and thereby humiliated in public (Bhuiyan, 2023). As a result, the Federal Trade Commission (FTC) has forbidden Rite Aid from using this technology for five years (Bhuiyan, 2023).

▶▶▶▶ When paired with facial recognition software, video from cameras in stores, restaurants, banks, schools, and other public places can help to track an individual. Law enforcement uses facial recognition to investigate crimes and, during the pandemic, to track down people who left their homes during lockdowns. School districts also use cameras and facial recognition software to analyze people approaching their schools to promote safer schools. Does this violate one's privacy, and are the school-safety benefits worth the sacrifice? Consider the questions and ask your students to consider the ethical tradeoffs of this technology, as well. This just shows the importance of really thinking and helping students think about what and where they are posting information and what happens to it beyond that initial placement. AI4ALL offers a free lesson for educators to teach students about facial recognition (**Figure 2.1**).

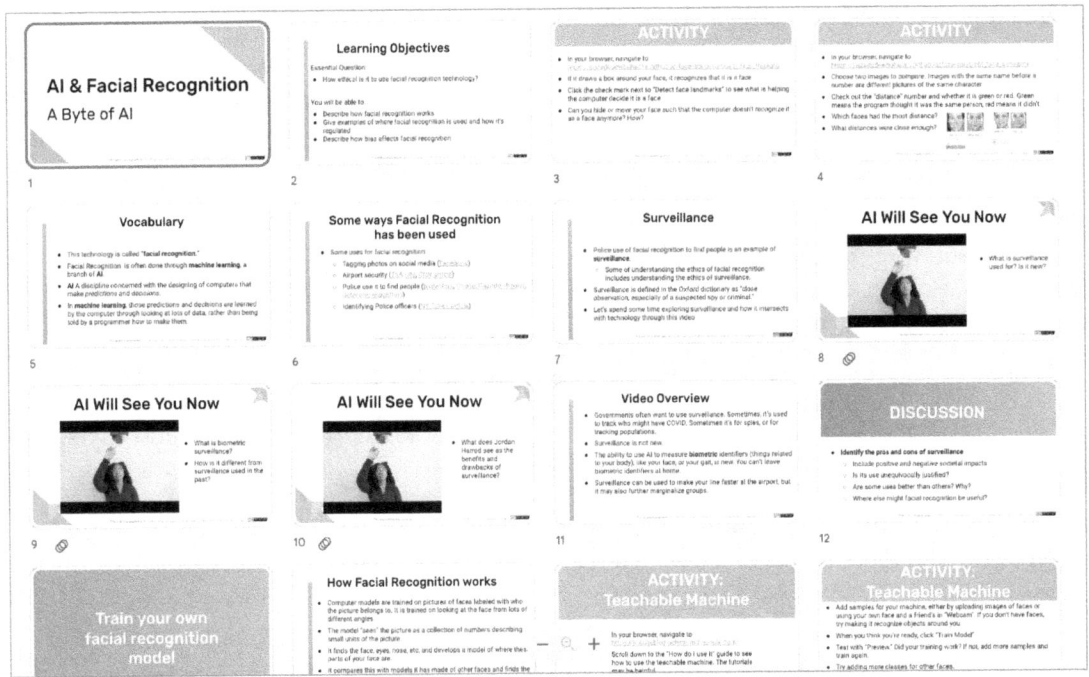

FIGURE 2.1

AI4ALL offers slides with content and embedded videos for teaching a lesson about facial recognition.

Helping Students Protect Their Privacy

▶▶▶▶ So, as educators how do we help students understand how best to protect their privacy? Start with a conversation. For example, you could ask students about their experiences when completing a survey or tell them to look for monitoring cameras when they go out in public. Depending on the age group you teach, you could discuss their social media use: What type of information do they share, and do they choose settings that keep their information set to private? When they search for information using Google, do they then notice ads related to their searches popping up on other sites they visit? Ask them why they think that is and how it happens.

Follow up your conversations about students' experiences with discussions about best practices for safeguarding privacy, such as the importance of reading websites' fine print to determine what data is collected and how it is used. Are companies and organizations selling our personal information to other third parties? Or have computers already been programmed to take our information and exchange it? Understanding exactly what happens to the data that we are sharing is vital. A few more questions to consider when thinking about what happens to all of the data are:

✦ Who is behind the programming of the AI tool?

✦ Who is collecting the data, and how are they then using it?

✦ What type of information is being collected? Is it personal information, such as names, age, and locations?

✦ Is the data collection in alignment with the relevant privacy laws, especially when it comes to children who are under the age requirement of some of these tools?

That last question must be considered by educators and education leaders, as well. It is critical that we make sure that student data is protected from any potential data breaches or from unauthorized access. Data protection protocols, such as encryption of data, need to be in place, making sure that the servers are secure, reminding students and educators about the importance of strong passwords, and using two-factor authentication.

Steps to Take

Helping students understand how to share their information responsibly and to protect themselves when interacting online has long been a part of digital citizenship lessons. Take a moment to think of how digital citizenship has changed because of AI and what AI tools are capable of. What skills are needed now, and how can we best help students develop them? It is important to have a consistent policy in place as well as standard procedures that are followed. Here are some steps you and your school can take.

✦ **Be proactive.** Gather resources and anticipate questions and concerns that educators, students, and their families may have.

✦ **Engage in conversations.** Make time to discuss potential issues. Invite stakeholders to discuss any issues that arise with regard to technology use, especially AI and generative AI.

Setting clear policies and guidelines about rapidly evolving technology like AI is important, but knowing how to begin can be difficult. An important first step is to involve different members of the school community in conversations about AI and any concerns, challenges, or needs. When considering guidelines or policies to implement, having these key stakeholders as part of a committee is essential.

Look at some example policies for inspiration, and consult resources such as the *Artificial Intelligence and the Future of Teaching and Learning: Insights and Recommendations* policy report from the United States Department of Education Office of Educational Technology. The report is quite helpful for educators to understand how to work with AI in education and to think about school technology plans and policies. Likewise, the TeachAI initiative offers an AI Guidance for Schools Toolkit that schools can use to guide discussions, evaluate policies, understand the impact of AI, and make sure that they are addressing all potential concerns that teachers, students, and their families may have. ISTE also has a great resource for helping school leaders understand AI and how to develop policy in their schools: the *Bringing AI to School: Tips for School Leaders* guide includes key definitions, examples, and some FAQs to provide suggested answers to common questions.

More resources may be on the way, too. The Executive Order on "safe, secure, and trustworthy artificial intelligence" also called for support for educators as they seek to create learning opportunities for students and bring AI-powered tools into the classroom. In it, the President directed action to "shape AI's potential to transform education by creating resources to support educators deploying AI-enabled educational tools, such as personalized tutoring in schools" (The White House, 2023).

With the rapid advancements we are seeing with AI, there will be innovation and transformation happening in our schools. While considering policies to address this, be sure to make time for professional development to discuss any changes that may impact instruction. We need to be prepared and ready to adjust. Creating policies and having access to the right resources will help us embrace the technology while also providing security for educators and students.

+ **Set clear policies and guidelines.** Review current school policies related to technology use, such as an Acceptable Use Policy (AUP) and other technology-related guidelines in place. Also review the protections set for the school network to make sure the tools and websites used are in compliance with school policies and laws related to technology use and student privacy. (See the sidebar "Policy Setting Guidance" for tips and resources.)

+ **Obtain consent.** Provide a form for signed parental consent that explains the type of technology that will be used, how it will be used, and if any data will be collected and how it will be shared or stored. It is critical that parents understand how data may be collected.

- **Update school network security.** Continue to update policies and systems as technology changes. The IT department should safeguard its server to protect educators and students. By using secure platforms for the exchange of information and transmitting student data, we will better protect all students.

- **Provide training and learning opportunities.** Include opportunities for educators to receive training provided by the school or to seek their own professional learning that is relevant to their content and needs. The training should also focus on how to identify and address bias and other ethical concerns with AI use.

To get started, you can turn to a lot of great resources available from national and international organizations (see the "Resources for Teaching About Ethics and AI" section and Appendix B for more details). These organizations provide teachers with resources they need to build comfort and confidence in discussing AI ethics. The biggest step is recognizing the importance of learning about ethics and making time for engaging in discussions.

Resources for Teaching About Ethics and AI

Teaching students about ethics and AI:

- Prepares them for the future

- Empowers them to become responsible AI users and advocates for ethical AI development and deployment

- Equips them with the critical thinking and problem-solving skills necessary to navigate the ethical challenges that artificial intelligence can bring

- Builds awareness of different perspectives and experiences

But with a topic so vast, where do you start? With the help of the resources and activities in this section, you can learn more about teaching ethics and AI to students, as well as how to engage students in meaningful discussions about the ethical dimensions of AI. These resources can be trusted because the listed organizations have vetted their materials and focus on privacy, security, and accuracy of information.

Online Courses

You can find a variety of courses and learning experiences to help educators develop skills related to AI. (Some can even be used with your students.) Many of the courses cover the basics of AI and then advance through various components of AI and also its ethical dilemmas. The courses offer a structured, self-paced learning experience by including activities, quizzes, readings, videos, and additional resources. Here are some to explore:

✦ **Code.org** created AI 101 in collaboration with ETS (Educational Testing Service), ISTE, and Khan Academy. The course is a free online learning series for educators. Additional resources for learning about AI are available through this site and course (**Figure 2.2**).

What is AI 101 for Teachers?

This is a free, foundational online learning series for any teacher and educator interested in the groundbreaking world of artificial intelligence (AI) and its transformative potential in education. Partners Code.org, ETS, ISTE and Khan Academy are offering engaging sessions with renowned experts that will demystify AI, explore responsible implementation, address bias, and showcase how AI-powered learning can revolutionize student outcomes. Join us on this journey of exploration and empowerment, and unlock the future of teaching with and about AI.

AVAILABLE NOW

Fireside Chat with Sal Khan and Hadi Partovi

Join Sal Khan (Khan Academy) and Hadi Partovi (Code.org) for a fireside chat on embracing artificial intelligence in the classroom. Expect a lively discussion including some of the most controversial topics surrounding AI today.

AVAILABLE NOW

Demystifying AI for Educators

Introduction to the fundamentals of Artificial Intelligence which will equip you with the foundational knowledge to understand the profound impact of AI in our society and its increasing relevance to the field of education.

📖 Companion guide: Large Language Model Prompts for Educators ↗

FIGURE 2.2
An example of some of the offerings for educators from the Code.org AI 101 course

- **Coursera** offers a free AI for Educators course for beginners. Available in nineteen languages, the course takes approximately sixteen hours to complete. The site also offers courses specific to ChatGPT, generative AI, and more advanced topics.

- **edX** offers a variety of courses focused on AI and also provides information related to obtaining degrees and certification in artificial intelligence.

- **ISTE U** offers their instructor-led Artificial Intelligence Explorations for Educators course in both English and Spanish. The course is a fifteen-hour course that provides educators with activities and resources to get started with learning and teaching about AI. ISTE also provides curriculum guides with lessons for educators to use in classrooms.

- **Khan Academy** offers a three-unit course for educators to learn about generative AI and how to teach with AI. It includes lesson plans from Common Sense Education covering topics such as bias, chatbots, facial recognition, and algorithms (**Figure 2.3**).

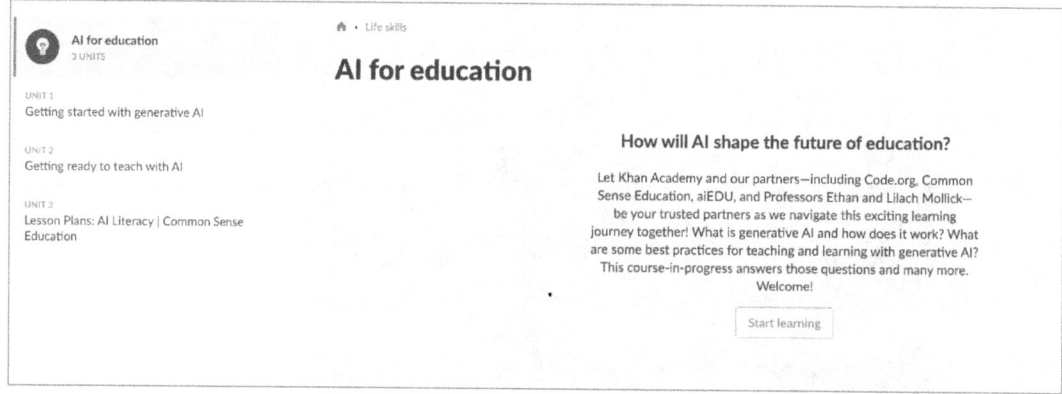

FIGURE 2.3
A generative AI course provided through Khan Academy in collaboration with Code.org, Common Sense Education, and AIEDU

- **Microsoft Educator Center** offers a short module for educators that explores the potential of AI (**Figure 2.4**). Additional AI-related courses and modules are also available.

- **Udemy** offers an introductory AI course called AI for Teachers and Educators. The course covers what AI is, key technologies, ethics, tips for using AI in the classroom, and what we might expect for the future.

FIGURE 2.4
Microsoft offers a course for educators to learn the potential of AI through their Educator Center.

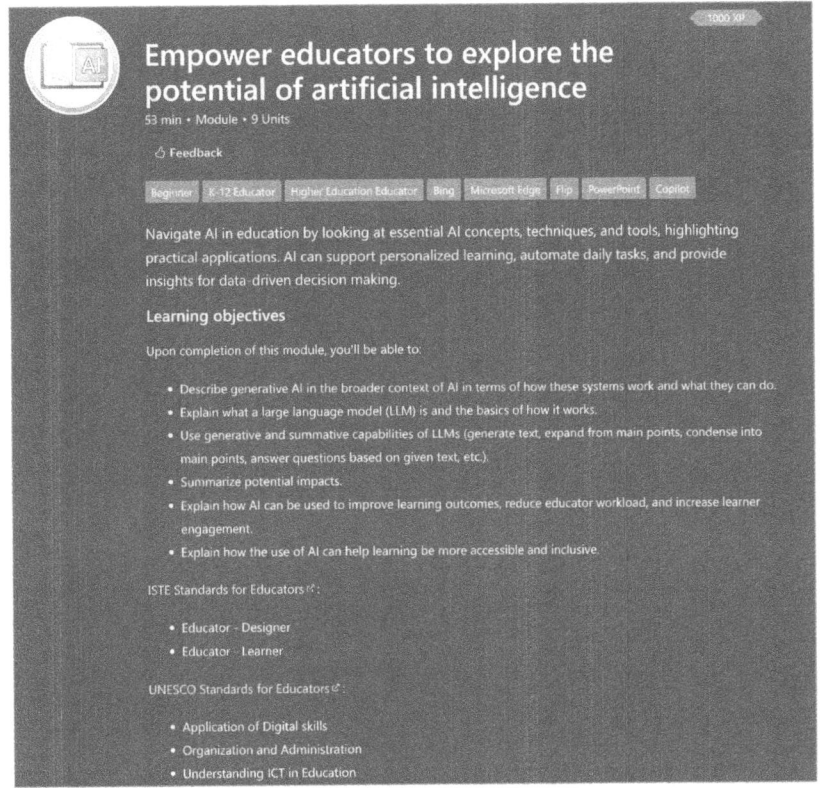

Educational Websites for AI and Ethics

Several organizations host websites dedicated to teaching AI ethics to students.

✦ **AI4ALL** offers several AI-focused lessons that include activities, objectives, slides, and videos. For example, the AI & Ethics lesson is a ten-hour learning opportunity for students to examine the ethical considerations that companies should focus on when creating AI-powered systems (**Figure 2.5**). It gives students an opportunity to create a company, collaborate, and innovate while learning about ethics. Other lesson topics include AI & Facial Recognition, AI & Deep Fakes, and AI & Drawing.

AI & Ethics Teaching Guide

AI and Ethics

This curriculum is an interactive deep dive into the sort of ethical concerns that companies creating AI based systems should consider. Students explore these ideas through role-playing running their own companies and making ethical decisions for those companies.

Standards:
For more information about
- **Common Core** - CCSS.ELA-LITERACY.RI.11-12.5, CCSS.ELA-LITERACY.RST.11-12.2, CCSS.ELA-LITERACY.RST.11-12.4, CCSS.ELA-LITERACY.RST.11-12.10, CCSS.ELA-LITERACY.SL.11-12.1, CCSS.ELA-LITERACY.SL.11-12.2, CCSS.ELA-LITERACY.SL.11-12.4, CCSS.ELA-LITERACY.WHST.11-12.2, CCSS.ELA-LITERACY.WHST.11-12.4, CCSS.ELA-LITERACY.WHST.11-12.5, CCSS.ELA-LITERACY.WHST.11-12.9, CCSS.ELA-LITERACY.W.11-12.2, CCSS.ELA-LITERACY.W.11-12.4, CCSS.ELA-LITERACY.W.11-12.5, CCSS.ELA-LITERACY.W.11-12.9
- **NGSS** - HS-ETS1-1, HS-ETS1-2
- **CSTA** - 2-IC-20, 3A-IC-29, 3A-IC-30, 2-IC-21, 3A-IC-24, 3B-IC-25
- **ISTE** - 2d, 3d, 4, 6
- **AI4K12 5 Big Ideas** - Learning, Impact

Time ~8 - 10 hours

How to use this curriculum:

This curriculum is most effective in an in-classroom setting where you can do group work and discussions.

In virtual classrooms students can do discussions on systems like Flipgrid or Padlet. You can organize times for groups to meet virtually. For more detailed virtual ideas, check out the online strategies guide.

Background:

✦ **AIEDU** is a non-profit organization that provides learning experiences and toolkits for advocates, learners, and teachers about AI literacy. In addition to a ten-week teacher-led course on AI (**Figure 2.6**), it offers free curriculum that includes challenges for students focused on ChatGPT, social media and its algorithms, and creating with generative AI. Teachers can select short-term projects for students in grades 9–12 that are self-guided and cover a range of topics such as algorithms used in Washington, D.C., facial recognition, the future of medicine with AI, and more (**Figure 2.7**). These projects encourage critical thinking and help students to explore topics of interest related to AI.

FIGURE 2.6
One of the resources available for educators is a ten-week program for students in grades 9–12 to learn about AI.

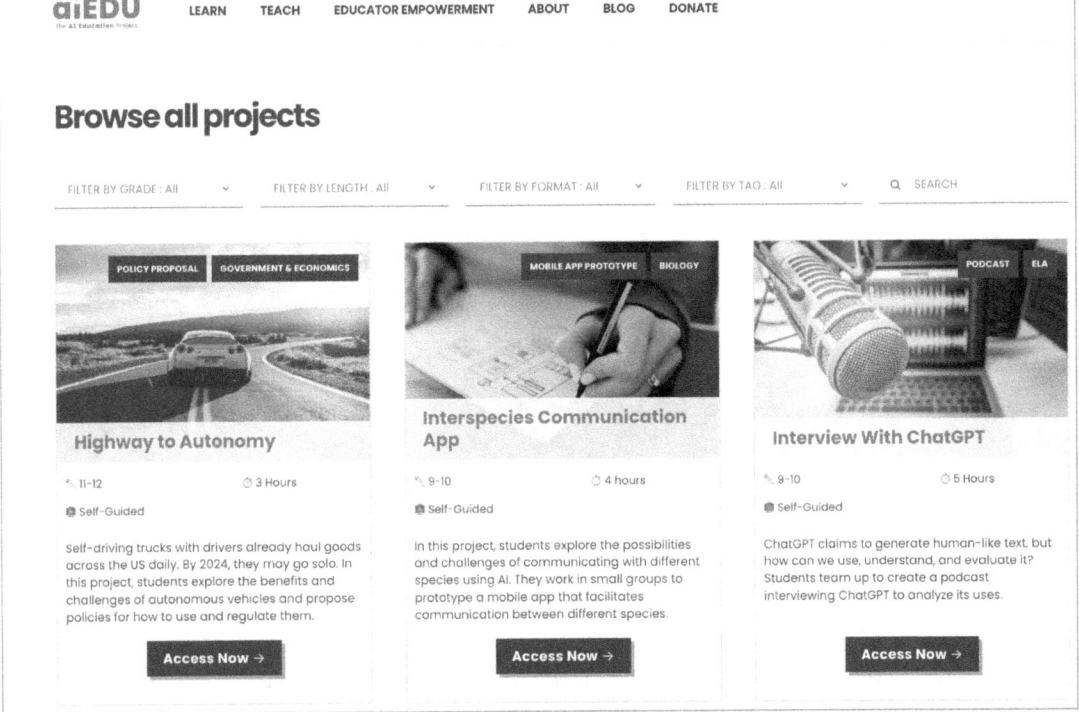

FIGURE 2.7
AIEDU offers lessons available for students to learn about AI via different content areas and topics, such as biology, ELA, and policy discussions.

✦ **AI4K12**, which is sponsored by the Association for Advancement of Artificial Intelligence and the Computer Science Teachers Association, provides a variety of resources for educators and students to learn about artificial intelligence. You'll find activities, books, curriculum, lessons, research materials, videos, and even demos to explore AI-related activities. The site also offers a downloadable Five Big Ideas in Artificial Intelligence poster and progression charts designed to help you customize the Big Ideas for various grade bands when teaching (**Figure 2.8**).

FIGURE 2.8
AI4K12.org offers progression charts for each of the Five Big Ideas with activities for different grade bands.

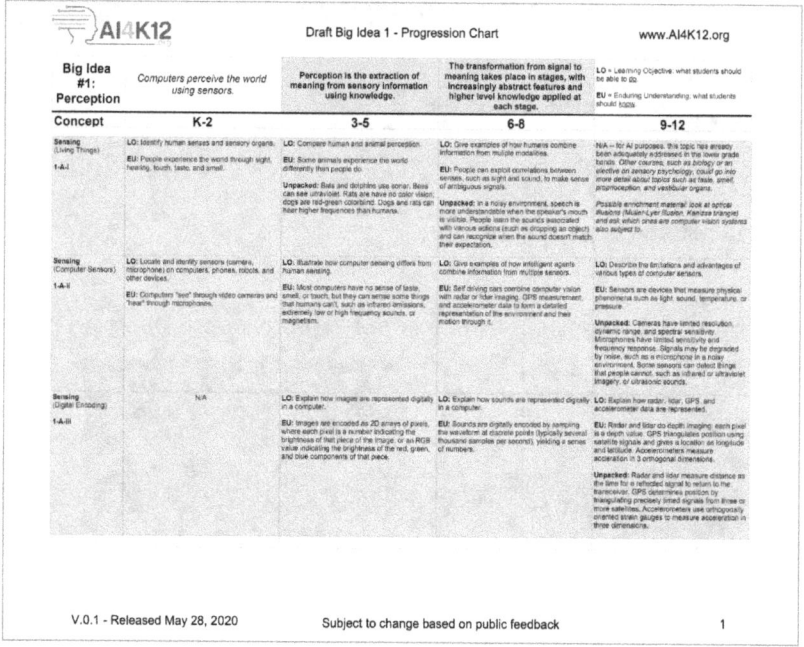

✦ **AI for Teachers** offers activities to help you learn how to bring artificial intelligence into your classroom. It provides lessons for students in grades K–5, 6–8, and 9–12 that progressively expand the complexity of activities that the students are engaging in with each grade band to topics including bias and ethics, autonomous vehicles, and more (**Figure 2.9**). For example, the Ethics and Artificial Intelligence Unit Plan is a comprehensive four-week plan with several focus areas that are great for students in grades 9–12 to explore, one of which involves students viewing a *Star Trek* video clip and then discussing an ethical dilemma. The audio and video resources in the unit plans provide interactive ways for students to process what AI is and how it works.

FIGURES 2.9
AI for Teachers offers a variety of lessons across multiple grade bands to help students learn about AI in real-world learning experiences.

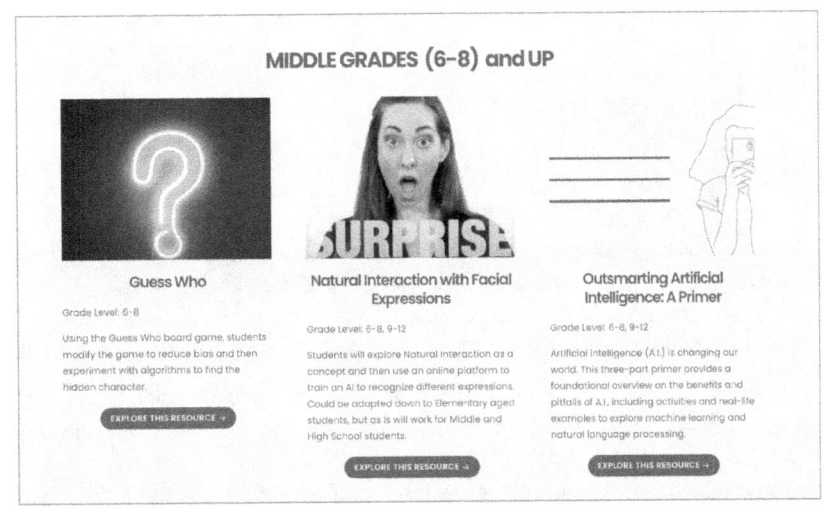

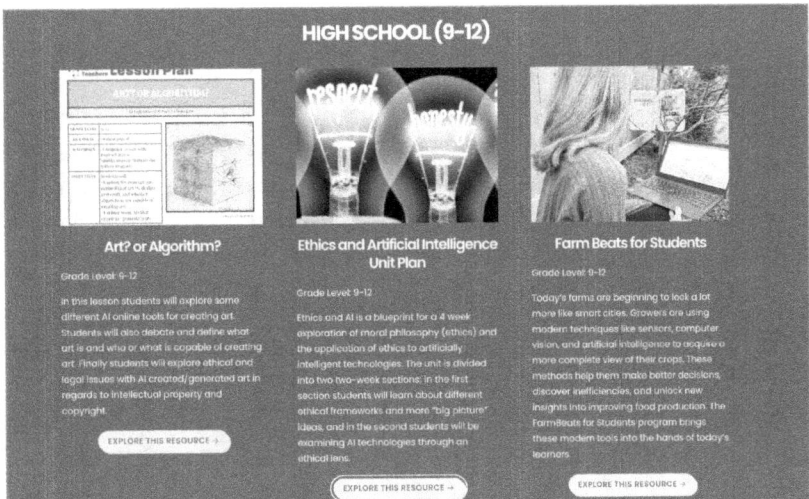

✦ **AI and Ethics from MIT** offers an open-source middle school curriculum for students to learn about ethics and artificial intelligence. Available in English, German, Korean, and Portuguese, the lessons include activities, assessments, supplemental materials, and teacher guides. You'll also find fun activities such as AI Bingo, a scavenger hunt focused on YouTube, and additional approaches to learning about bias and algorithms.

✦ **Code.org** houses a lot of great information, lessons, and videos for educators of all grade levels, including explanations about artificial intelligence and how it's used in the world. Featured topics include bias, ethics, machine learning, and more. Their AI 101 course, developed in partnership with ETS, ISTE, and Khan Academy, is free to teachers who want to learn more about AI and AI in education.

By Jérôme Nogues, Head of Digital and Innovation, Old Hall School, England

The ethical implications of using generative AI are of the utmost significance. I emphasize the necessity of prioritizing ethical and responsible practices while interacting with the capabilities of generative AI systems. Users and developers must both thoughtfully consider issues including responsibility, transparency, bias, and privacy. It is imperative that AI-generated content be used in ways that don't hurt people or reinforce unfair prejudice. We have a responsibility to aggressively address and correct any biases present in the training data. Additionally, it is morally required to respect intellectual property rights and obtain the proper consent for producing content.

I believe that teaching how to use AI should start early so that our pupils can understand its power but also learn to approach it critically and use it ethically. I incorporated a dedicated AI section into my curriculum, starting from the second grade (Y3 in the U.K.). The children greatly enjoyed my lesson on generative AI for creating images. I began by briefly introducing what generative AI is, and then we embarked on a project centered around Yayoi Kusama, the exceptionally original Japanese artist. I recommended the Tate gallery's Tate Kids YouTube channel as a valuable resource. Initially, we created real artwork inspired by Kusama's famous polka dots. I provided the children with templates of various household items, flowers, and vegetables, allowing them to choose one or even to combine two or three to design their own unique creations.

Once their artwork was completed, we transitioned to using Canva (which is free for educators), and I introduced its Text to Image features to the children. Recognizing that some students had writing challenges due to their age, I explained that they needed to compose a prompt to instruct the computer to create images. I presented a simple example on the board that they could use and modify: *Design a painting of a pumpkin in the style of Yayoi Kusama*. The outcomes were outstanding. They assembled a collage of their results and incorporated pictures of their own artwork. We then engaged in a discussion about the ethics of creating images using AI versus crafting their own artwork, fostering their critical thinking. We pondered whether it was fair to utilize AI to produce an image and then claim authorship.

✦ **Moral Machine** was created by MIT and gives you a chance to evaluate situations when it comes to ethics. You are presented with thirteen pairs of scenarios involving self-driving cars, and you have to decide which option to take in each. You also can see how others responded to each scenario.

✦ **TeachAI** provides the AI Guidance for Schools Toolkit, developed with collaboration from Code.org, ETS, ISTE, and Khan Academy. It provides support for school leaders, educators, and policymakers in developing guidance on the "safe, effective, and responsible" use of AI in their schools. In the Toolkit, you can find ideas for integrating AI, sample policies and guidance on revising policies, sample presentations on AI and its impact, benefits and concerns, as well as information for parents and students. Plus, the site offers links to a multitude of additional resources, plus webinars about the Toolkit.

For more information on available resources, scan the QR code at the end of this chapter or see Appendix B.

⚑ Activities: Addressing Ethical Dilemmas

With so many resources and important topics to cover when it comes to AI, finding the time to design a full lesson or determining how to make it relevant can be a challenge. One option is to use a lesson or a curriculum guide, such as ISTE's five *Hands-on AI Projects for the Classroom* guides (**Figure 2.10**).

FIGURE 2.10
The opening page of a project in ISTE's *Hands-on AI Projects for the Classroom: A Guide on Ethics and AI*

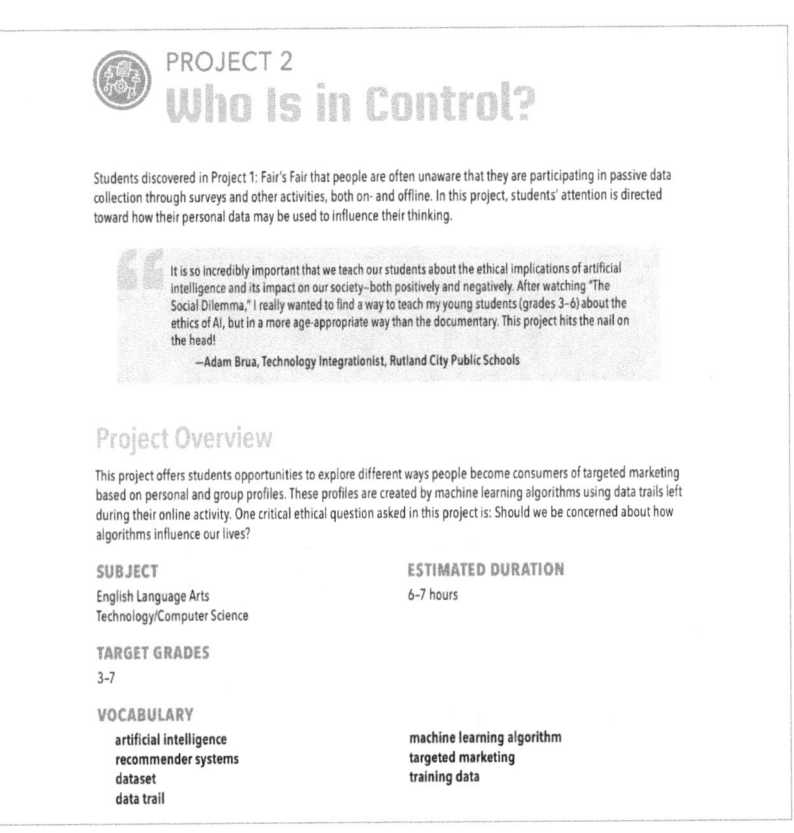

Each offers four ready-to-implement AI learning projects, and with guides for elementary, secondary, computer science, and elective educators, plus one focused on ethics and

AI, you can easily get started. Each project begins by listing relevant standards (ISTE Standards for Students, ISTE Computational Thinking Competencies, Common Core Standards, and AI4k12 Five Big Ideas), important definitions, and preparation materials, and then provides a full-lesson plan for class activities. These guides are great to use, and they're available as free downloads in Arabic, English, and Spanish.

Beyond those in the ISTE guides, here are some additional activities you can try to address ethics and AI in your classroom.

+ **Bias and AI:** Start by discussing the concept of bias. Ask students to share their ideas about how bias can impact people and lead to unfair treatment or discrimination. Divide students into small groups, and give them each a different type of AI technology, such as the use of facial recognition technology, automated decision-making systems, or something that the students suggest. Next, have students research the system, specifically exploring what potential for biases it holds. Each group should suggest solutions to mitigate the bias they found and decide how to share their information with their classmates. After each group shares, encourage students to engage in a full-class discussion to think about each group's findings and to come up with additional insights and suggestions for solutions to the ethical concerns they identified.

+ **Ethical dilemmas:** A good opportunity for students to work together is to divide them into groups and create scenarios for the students to explore. This will push their critical-thinking skills, build collaboration, and help them to think through and be involved in ethical discussions related to artificial intelligence. Present them with scenarios related to self-driving cars, chatbots being used for healthcare or therapy, or how algorithms may influence decisions and the impact of this. Have students work together to discuss and analyze any ethical implications of the scenario, think about the negative effects, and then brainstorm ideas and propose solutions to address the ethical dilemmas. Each group should then share their proposal. Finally, involve the whole class in a discussion or even a debate so that students can share their perspectives and extend the conversation.

+ **Guest speakers and panels:** Invite guest speakers who are working in AI-related fields and have experience with the ethical considerations involved. You can leverage your local community or reach out to your ISTE network or personal learning network (PLN) to locate a guest speaker for your classroom. Whether in person or through a video call, opportunities like this connect students with real-world insights and are more authentic and meaningful ways to learn about such an important topic. Students can ask questions to experts in the field, which may spark interest for them to explore future career opportunities.

✦ **Real-world scenarios:** In class, have discussions about AI and its use in the world. Ask students to look for professional or daily uses of AI and then analyze how it works, the impact it has, and if there are any ethical concerns related to it. Students can then share what they have learned and engage in an authentic and meaningful discussion, which also will promote critical thinking and problem-solving skills. If they identify concerns, task them with designing solutions, which will boost engagement and creativity.

✦ **Student projects:** Design learning experiences that involve students working together on AI ethics projects. For example, students could write a code of conduct to follow, do an audit of an AI-powered tool, or examine how AI is used in different areas of life and work. Ask students to present their findings and potential solutions to any ethical issues they identify.

Keep the Conversation Going

With students and our fellow educators, we must make ethics part of our conversations—not only in activities about artificial intelligence and its impact, but in all that we do. The many resources and discussion topics available can lead to rich and important conversations with our students. Choose an activity, try it with your students, and always make time to reflect on it and evaluate the impact on student understanding and learning. Ask students for their ideas about how the activity could be improved and how to explore ethics and AI. Give them an opportunity to create, innovate, and lead in your classroom.

Key Takeaways

Understanding the ethical concerns that can arise when bringing technology into the classroom, especially with the use of AI-powered tools, is critical for educators and students. Students must develop their digital citizenship skills and learn to interact in the online space. (*ISTE Standards 1.2.a, 1.2.d Digital Citizen*)

Educators have a responsibility to guide students in responsible and safe use of technology. Time for conversation and exploration of tools, privacy settings, and how information is used needs to be part of ongoing conversations and evaluation of school policies. (*ISTE Standards 1.1.d Empowered Learner, 1.3.d Knowledge Constructor, 1.4.d Innovative Designer, 1.5.d Computational Thinker*)

Finding the right resources to support educators and guide students is important, especially with the rapidly advancing technology available. Staying current with research, as well as mentoring and modeling the ethical and responsible use of these tools, is critical. (*ISTE Standards 2.2.a, 2.2.b, 2.2.c Leader, 2.3.c Citizen, 3.1.d Equity and Citizenship Advocate*)

tinyurl.com/ykt7c8z9

You can find additional resource suggestions in Appendix B or by scanning the QR code.

Questions for Reflection and Discussion

As you can see, ethics is a very important component of learning about and teaching about AI. There are many ways to present ethics in our classrooms, and fortunately, a variety of tools and organizations provide the support that educators need to get started, as well as resources that can be shared with families. Ethics should be part of ongoing conversations in our classrooms, especially as we see the advancements with AI and potentially other concerns arise. Before we dive in to the impact of AI on education, take a moment to reflect on what you've learned throughout this chapter.

✦ How can educators ensure that AI in education remains equitable and accessible to all students, regardless of their backgrounds or abilities?

✦ What are some additional ideas you have for lessons focused on ethics?

✦ How might real-world case studies of AI-related ethical issues encourage students to think critically about the implications of AI technologies?

✦ How can discussions about the ethics of AI foster empathy and global awareness among students?

✦ In your school, what policies are in place to deal with academic integrity or to regularly evaluate tools and look for any ethical concerns? Could they be enhanced? What would you recommend after reading this chapter?

Share your ideas with me on X (formerly Twitter) @Rdene915 or post a message on LinkedIn.

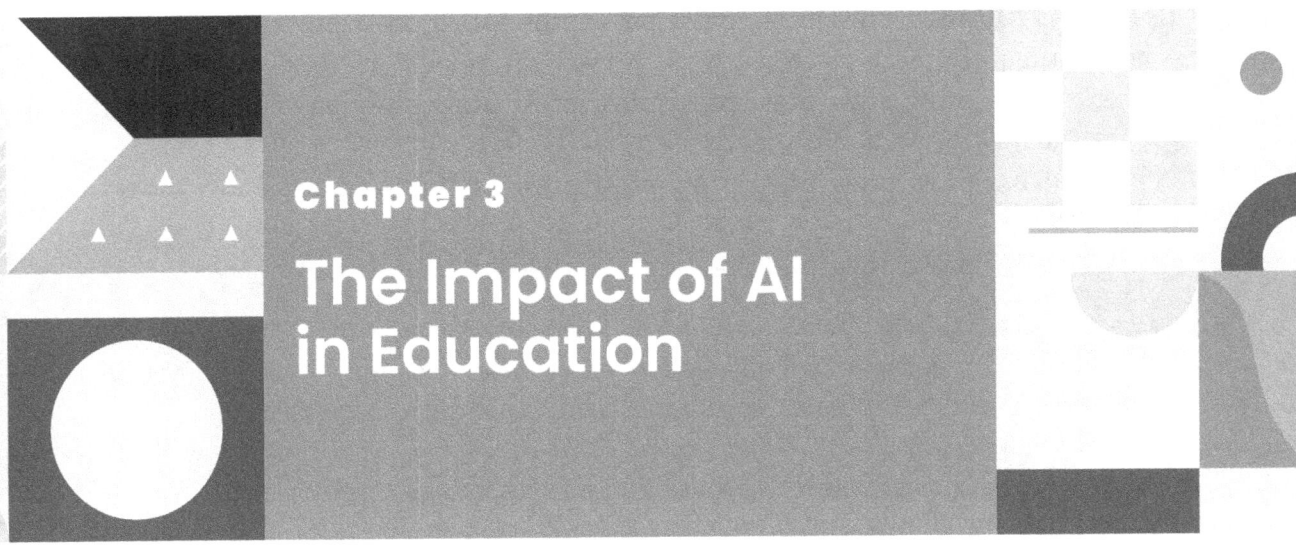

The content of this chapter aligns with the following standards and indicators:

ISTE Student Standards

1.1.d Empowered Learner

1.3.b Knowledge Constructor

ISTE Educator Standards

2.1.c Learner

2.2.c Leader

2.3.b Citizen

2.4.b Collaborator

IN RECENT YEARS, artificial intelligence has become a hot topic of conversation, but AI is not anything new. For years, educators have been using tools that are powered by AI technology—in most cases, without even realizing it—to access information, streamline tasks, customize instruction, and more. The time has come to be more receptive to and intentional in our use of technology because it will continue to evolve, and "AI-supported instruction is expected to transform education" (Celik et al., 2023). If we choose to avoid it in our classrooms, we will be doing a disservice to students.

So we need to be ready to embrace the changes, whether or not we want to. Think of it as an opportunity to build your own skills and to learn with and from your students. If you feel as though you're not prepared, don't worry. This chapter will help you get ready to bring AI opportunities to students as well as learn about how these tools will impact the work of educators. While Chapter 2 discussed ethical concerns regarding AI and academic integrity, here we'll discuss how AI can enhance communication, personalize learning, facilitate student exploration, differentiate instruction, create adaptive assessments that provide tailored feedback and support to each student, as well as help you create more engaging and effective learning experiences for your students (and save you time doing so).

The Big Disruptor

Offering a freely available and easy way to create content, the arrival of OpenAI's ChatGPT in November of 2022 "put an intense spotlight on generative AI systems and their possible impacts on academic integrity" (Eke, 2023) and caused great concern and uncertainty among educators. I received many phone calls, emails, and messages asking if I thought that schools should ban ChatGPT. Wouldn't the possible outcomes be too dangerous—easy plagiarism, creativity atrophy, a loss of critical thinking skills? My answer was, and still is, "No." Gill et al. agree, writing that "limiting or forbidding ChatGPT won't solve the problem. It is preferable to accept it and establish explicit guidelines for its application in academic settings" (2024, p. 23).

When it comes to something that's going to disrupt our educational system, I believe we need to take time to learn about it, explore it, evaluate it, and really think about its impact. Are its benefits great enough to outweigh its negatives, and if so, how do we embrace it? The most important thing to do is seek to understand before deciding to avoid it. Avoiding ChatGPT or other AI tools in our classrooms does not mean that students will avoid using them outside of school. Instead, we need to engage in conversations and seek opportunities to help students and ourselves learn about what AI (or any other emerging technology) is capable of.

Within the first week of ChatGPT being available, for example, I spent a few hours testing out prompts of all types at home and then explored it in class the next day with my eighth-grade students. Together we came up with prompts and had fun exploring its capabilities, but we also took time to analyze and evaluate it to better understand its limitations. We discussed how it could potentially be used to benefit learners or people in any area of work they do. We tried to decide if the output sounded human or not and how we could tell. Opportunities like this to analyze the output from AI are important ways to help students build their analytical and critical thinking skills.

As educators, we must continue to rethink our instructional practices so that we can stay current and relevant as technology changes. We have to think about what we are asking our students to do that will provide them with higher-level skills rather than solely relying on information generated by AI. If they can simply get answers from Google or find answers already made by AI, we are not asking the right questions. Students must apply the knowledge they gain and then extend their thinking. The key question we must ask ourselves is: How can we leverage what AI does well without taking away opportunities from students to develop their skills and creating a reliance on technology that may disappear entirely?

What Does AI Mean for Today's Classrooms?

AI has been referred to as a game changer for education. Its capabilities can transform learning experiences and the way that teachers provide instruction for their students, ranging "from assessment design to language learning" (Gill et al., 2024, p. 20). To provide their students with timely feedback and personalized learning, for example, many K–12 teachers already use AI to automatically grade assessments, provide feedback via chatbots, or supply data analytics that identify areas of student learning needs. The use of AI-powered tools like these saves valuable time for teachers. Because we can quickly assess students using AI technology, we gain more time to then work directly with students individually, to provide materials that are specific to their learning needs, and to progress at a pace that works the best for them. Using AI-powered digital assessment and grading tools helps teachers provide more timely feedback to students, while the time saved opens more opportunities to spend with students one on one or with whole-class instruction. With AI as a "virtual assistant," teachers are freed to move around the room and facilitate learning. (For specific ideas, see the section "Tools for Teachers" later in this chapter.)

With AI tools, students have access to new ways of learning and obtaining information. A study by Gill et al. identified benefits of having ChatGPT serve as a virtual instructor for students, concluding that it "may help learners with their web-based independent research by responding to their inquiries and can improve collaboration by offering suggestions for a debate framework and giving immediate response" (2024, p. 22). When using adaptive learning platforms, students receive the support they need, right when they need it. AI tools become a personal tutor. Chatbots, for example, provide opportunities for students to interact and ask questions. A chatbot taking on the role of a Spanish speaker could help a to cite sources and check facts, especially when using tools like ChatGPT. As part of our technology program, we have many discussions on the benefits and concerns of using all types of technology. We discuss digital citizenship, media literacy, and cyberbullying using Common Sense Media's AI literacy lessons for grades 6–12.

Last year, my school celebrated the Day of AI for the first time, and I loved the resources available to teachers. On **dayofai.org**, you can find curriculum, slide decks, tutorials, and lesson plans ready to go to engage students of all ages. It allows for those discussions on benefits and risks.

I have also found that modeling the use of AI tools in my classes is a great way to show students how to use the technology appropriately. I like to share how I use MagicSchool.ai, Curipod, and similar tools to create lessons. I have shown my students how I can search for and enter prompts to find what I need, as well as how I check the material before I present it to them. Not all the information may be correct or in line with what is in the text that we are using, so I have to make adjustments. They also love it when I can quickly incorporate a brain break or a joke in the middle of a lesson. They see how AI saves time and makes learning more engaging for them. I can also adapt lessons for different learning styles and differentiate my lessons to meet the needs of all students.

In addition, I like to share how I created an AI-generated image in Canva to go along with a lesson, and then challenge my students to use the AI tool to design a school poster. We talk about how to enter information into the prompt and how adding details will generate even better images. They learn the importance of entering correct information and being clear when writing a prompt for AI tools. We have had many valuable conversations—and some laughs when working with AI.

I enjoy sharing tools and sites with my colleagues, as well. It's exciting to see ways they are using them and the discussions that ensue. Together, we are continuing to reap the benefits of the many AI tools for teachers and students and keeping the conversations going on best practices and uses.

student build confidence in speaking skills. If a student was preparing for a job interview or oral exam, a chatbot could generate practice questions and even provide feedback to help the student build their skills. It is these types of opportunities where learners can leverage the AI-powered tools to help them develop skills like confidence initially, and then become more comfortable with tasks such as speaking and interacting with others.

Given the broad reach of AI's capabilities, you may wonder whether AI will lead to the replacement of teachers or at least take away opportunities from students to develop relationships with classmates and teachers. AI is not, and should not, be allowed to become a substitute for building relationships and human interaction. Although it can replace some of the *tasks* that we do, it cannot replace the human component of our work. Students need authentic and meaningful feedback and the human interactions that only we can provide.

Knowing our students' specific needs is key. AI is just another tool that we can leverage to help us work with our students more closely, to be able to identify their needs faster, and to provide exactly what they need when they need it. The key is understanding it and knowing how to use it in appropriate, ethical, and responsible ways.

We have to model the responsible practice of using these tools in our classrooms for students. They learn from us how these tools can be used, their benefits, their drawbacks, and the ways to minimize the risks and ethical dilemmas we discussed in Chapter 2. We need to find a balance in using this technology so that it helps students rather than hinders their learning or leads to a decrease in interpersonal skills and relationship building in our classroom community. We also need to help students learn about the impact of these tools (both good and bad) and how they may impact their future. (See Chapter 6 for more information about the future of work with AI.) AI is here, and its use and presence is growing. We need to embrace it, even if cautiously at first.

When students are in our classrooms learning with us, for example, we can engage with them, interact, provide feedback, and offer support to help them along their learning journey. When students have questions or seek feedback when we are not available, on the other hand, we can use AI tools to bridge the gap. Providing that access is essential for keeping the learning going.

How? Let's take a look at the ways AI can enhance some common learning scenarios:

- **Personalized learning:** AI-powered adaptive learning platforms can quickly analyze a student's strengths, identify areas where they need extra support, track their learning preferences, and design an appropriate assessment. They can show a student's mastery of the content, repeat lessons as needed, and quickly design a personalized learning plan for each student at their pace. These tools also can track the student's pace in learning and provide real-time support and additional content to meet their specific learning needs. The ability of AI to provide real-time feedback to students is helpful, especially when students are not working in the classroom. It can help students to keep working toward their learning goals. Teachers can do this, but AI can expand the when, how, and where of learning.

- **Practicing for confidence:** The use of interactive chatbots can help students build confidence in learning by simulating real conversations. Through AI technology, the chatbot can adapt to students' proficiency levels, thus providing one-on-one support. As a language educator, I often see students hesitate to speak in front of others. The fear of making mistakes and failure leads students to hold back and can also increase stress in learning. Practicing with a chatbot that can provide feedback can minimize that performance anxiety to build comfort and confidence over time. It is also useful for practicing for interviews or preparing for assessments. Students have even used ChatGPT to generate practice questions for their own quizzes or interviews.

✦ **Multimodal learning:** Some AI-powered tools provide multiple modes of interaction, including speech recognition for speaking practice, translation, and language learning capabilities; generating visual aids for vocabulary building; and generating many other types of content. Students can input text prompts to ask the AI tool to create an image, audio, or video, or they can use a prompt to obtain or clarify information in a specific format that meets their needs. Students who need to write essays or who struggle with specific types of questions can use a chatbot or tool like ChatGPT as a study buddy. (Remind them, however, of the need to be mindful of the information's accuracy.)

✦ **Accessible learning:** Many resources are available to help students who may have audio or visual impairments. AI caption generators can add captions to audiovisual content to promote access for all students, for example, and Microsoft's free app Seeing AI promotes accessibility in several ways. Seeing AI can analyze a scene, an object, a person, and more, and then use speech to describe what is seen. Amazon's Alexa and Apple's Siri respond to voice activation and carry out requested tasks. Nuance's Dragon Speech Recognition Solutions can transcribe up to 160 spoken words per minute and has voice commands for navigating documents with a 99% accuracy rate. PCEye from Tobii Dynavox is an eye-tracking device that enables its user to communicate and control a computer through eye movements; in the demonstration I saw, it assisted a young woman who had multiple sclerosis. The Otter app can transcribe speech into notes and summarize that content to assist learners—another way to provide more differentiation in far less time.

AI Impact for Learners

AI tools can benefit student learning in many ways, and we can learn much from our students' viewpoints. Here are six ways that AI can have a positive impact (McClennen & Poth 2022):

✦ **Adaptive learning:** Learning can be frustrating at times, and students, especially young ones, need opportunities to build their skills and to refine areas where they need extra help. In an adaptive learning model, students receive content that meets their specific needs and abilities and that enables them to learn at a pace that is comfortable to them. *Adaptive learning platforms* use AI algorithms to analyze students' strengths and weaknesses and then tailor educational content to each student's individual needs, reinforcing concepts they struggle with and challenging them in areas where they excel. These tools are not a replacement for the teacher-student interaction and the authentic and meaningful feedback loop, but they can supplement it. For example, the DreamBox Math and DreamBox Reading platforms work to enhance mathematical and literacy skills, providing content and extra practice that meets a student's specific needs, right when they need it (**Figure 3.1**). Similarly, Prodigy Math uses AI to create personalized math lessons and practice activities for students. Some common game-based learning tools already include AI enhancements. With Quizizz, for example, students recognize that they are building their skills during the activity as it adapts to their needs in real time, providing extra practice in areas where it is needed. In higher education, Knewton is a popular adaptive learning platform.

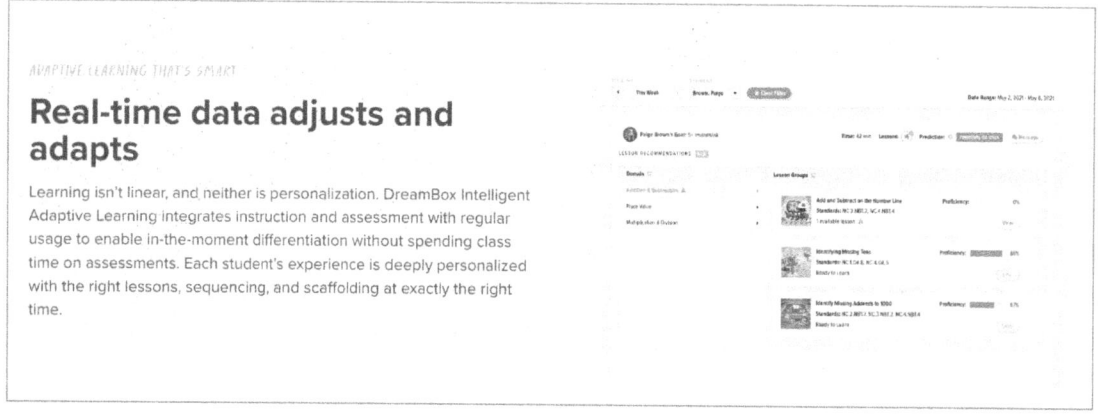

AVAPTIVE LEARNING THAT'S SMART

Real-time data adjusts and adapts

Learning isn't linear, and neither is personalization. DreamBox Intelligent Adaptive Learning integrates instruction and assessment with regular usage to enable in-the-moment differentiation without spending class time on assessments. Each student's experience is deeply personalized with the right lessons, sequencing, and scaffolding at exactly the right time.

FIGURE 3.1
DreamBox Learning offers more personalized learning experiences for students through its adaptive learning platform. Students work through lessons, and the platform provides differentiation for each student.

✦ **Feedback:** Many AI-powered tools can provide feedback directly to learners in real time. When a student completes an activity, such as a game-based assessment, the tool can identify areas that the learner needs to work on and help them to master the content better and even faster. Or, a student can ask a chatbot for specific feedback on something that they have written. In both instances, AI keeps the learning going, supporting students and keeping them on track with their learning goals. These tools can also help students develop essential social-emotional learning (SEL) skills like self-awareness, to know where they are in their learning process and self-management, and to work through challenges and set learning goals.

✦ **Content retention:** AI tools can offer multiple methods of reviewing material and help students build their skills in ways that meet their interests and that are available to them when they need it. Because the AI functionality is able to sort through the data and design a more personalized learning experience, students get the repetition they need to help them better retain the content—real-time support when they need it. Quizlet, for example, offers AI functionality that adapts to students' progress and can identify areas for students where they need further review—another way to help students build skills in self-awareness. Quizlet also has Q-Chat, the "first fully adaptive, AI-powered tutor experience built on OpenAI's ChatGPT API" (Quizlet, 2023), which provides personalized feedback to help students strengthen their understanding and retention of key concepts.

✦ **Language learning:** Chatbots powered by natural language processing (NLP) algorithms can engage students in interactive conversations, provide instant feedback, and create opportunities that enable students to build skills at their own pace. For example, Duolingo's chatbots enable students to build world language skills through conversational exercises. Students feel as though they are having a conversation with a human and can build confidence and comfort in speaking and interacting in the target language. As students speak, the AI analyzes their pronunciation to then assess and provide feedback. Also, AI-powered translation tools like Google Translate and Microsoft Immersive Reader enable students to explore and compare different languages, which can be a highly engaging activity done in any grade level simply for exploration. Newsela promotes accessibility and uses AI to adapt the reading materials to meet students' reading levels, which makes comprehension more accessible and enjoyable. An audio-visual vocabulary app for language learners, Knowji uses algorithms to track learner progress, can anticipate when a learner is going to forget a word, and can provide repetition and additional practice.

✦ **Social-emotional learning:** Building interpersonal and social skills can be challenging at times for students, and learning how to have a conversation by engaging with a chatbot can be a fun opportunity to strengthen those skills while learning about AI. While building content skills and conversational confidence, students can build SEL skills in the process. Check out resources from the IBM Developer Course or MIT App Inventor for examples in action.

- **Virtual tutoring:** Depending on the student's age, they may be able to access chatbots and ask questions. The chatbot then serves as their virtual assistant or tutor. Students working on an assignment in the evening, over the weekend, or any time they don't have instant access to their classroom teacher can turn to some of these AI-powered tools. They can ask questions and receive just enough information to help them continue in their learning journey. Being able to access help when and as often as needed is key.

For even more AI-powered platforms that benefit students, see Alex McFarland's article "10 Best AI Tools for Education" (**unite.ai/10-best-ai-tools-for-education**) and Appendix B.

AI Impact for Educators

Considering the work that we do in our classrooms, we are involved in a lot of different planning that focuses on assessing our students, building relationships, and developing methods and activities to help students learn and master content. AI and the growing number of tools available can help us streamline the workflow in this process. Not only can it help amplify the learning potential of students, but it can also enable teachers to provide more in less time. We can then use that reclaimed time in more effective ways for the benefit of students. Here are some areas where AI-powered tools can help educators:

- **Assessments:** As educators, we need to be able to evaluate our students so we can understand where they are in the learning process, but this can be quite time consuming, depending on the format of the assessment. We need to understand their strengths and areas where they need additional help so that we can target our instruction and differentiate to meet each student's needs. Because AI can process and analyze large amounts of data efficiently and in relatively little time, AI-powered tools can help you assess students and streamline the grading process, leaving you more time for classroom interactions. AI-powered assessment tools can design personalized learning paths and generate questions in real time, providing students with more targeted support to help them build skills. Students can use these tools whenever they need to, receiving support that meets their specific needs and abilities as they are working through various tasks.

  - When giving assessments such as standardized tests, assisted by AI-powered tools, educators gain insight into student progress faster and can act upon it to provide better learning experiences for students. The tools can also provide more consistency in grading assessments, minimizing bias and preventing mistakes in grading by the teacher (it happens, trust me). This results in improved student learning outcomes and enables teachers to give students more authentic, meaningful, and timely feedback.

- ▪ When I use AI to create quick assessments in my class, I openly tell my students that I am using AI-generated questions. You can ask ChatGPT, for example, to create a quiz, a rubric, discussion questions, project ideas, and so much more. (We will talk about ChatGPT in depth in Chapter 4.)

✦ **Differentiation:** With the availability of AI, students and teachers can connect with resources they need exactly when they need them. These resources are deliverable to each student, which saves valuable time for more interaction between teacher and student, and among students. Through AI, students can have instant access to one-to-one tutors, creating more authentic learning experiences by pairing students with an expert or a virtual peer identified based on an assessment of the student's needs and error analyses. As students work through a lesson and have questions, the virtual tutor can work with them as a guide, to keep the learning going.

- ▪ ▶▶▶▶ There are many ways to use AI tools for differentiation. For example, you could prompt ChatGPT to quickly create a list of eight ways for students to show learning for your class. AI-based tools can even generate differentiated rubrics for an assignment that will help you provide more options for students. You can then choose the best options to meet students where they are in terms of needs and interests, thereby enhancing the learning journey for every student.

✦ **Efficiency and productivity:** An issue that comes up a lot when I speak with educators is how much time it takes to complete communication tasks: sending emails, writing newsletters, creating new presentations for our students, and more. All of these take time away from working with students more closely or engaging in our own learning and professional growth. Generative AI tools can facilitate communication by creating audio, images, presentations, and video from a text prompt—not to mention automating repetitive tasks. Educators need to design a variety of materials for classes. AI can help us save time creating these, enabling us to focus on things that matter like time with our students.

✦ **Exploration:** Through generative AI, you and your students can find resources instantly based on a student's personal interest or for the entire class to experience. These resources will not be limited to a generated text description; AI can generate images or an interactive simulation, for example, to show students what they want to explore and potentially spark further interest in learning about different topics based on what AI has compiled.

+ **Personalization:** What better way to offer more personalized learning opportunities for students than to have AI analyze student responses, determine areas of need and interest, and find resources or create new questions to help students better understand the content? AI can help inform classroom teachers, enabling them to work together to create new learning opportunities for students, but faster and in a way that relates directly to student needs and offers authentic and timely feedback. Because of its algorithms, AI is capable of analyzing the way that people learn and their preferences and use these to create a personalized learning journey. It can provide customized recommendations for additional activities or recommend additional study materials. Access to resources available through AI can help to make learning more accessible for students and reduce the time and cost that it takes to gather other resources.

Tools for Teachers

Consider a common scenario: You want to do a quick check on how well students are mastering the content that you recently covered in class. You want them to respond to questions but also to provide you with feedback through open-ended responses. You could, of course, use a worksheet or a survey tool as a pulse check, but these methods would require you to take time to write out the questions or design the survey—time you don't have. A quicker solution? Leverage AI technology to generate a quick assessment or a survey in seconds or a few minutes. AI can even provide teachers with a virtual teaching assistant (something that was done in 2015 without students even knowing), which then frees time for them to move around the room and facilitate learning. Today there are educators relying on ChatGPT as a pseudo teaching assistant to save time with some clerical tasks. Again, consider what tasks take time away from your students and then test out some tools to see if you can supplement what you are providing with AI-generated content or AI-powered assessment tools.

To help you with this task and more, here are thirteen tools that I have tested and recommend for generating content and assessing students. Many of these I use regularly in my classroom or for working with other educators.

✦ **Canva Magic Studio** is a suite of AI tools that combine to provide quite a versatile platform for creating a variety of content types. Magic Write, for example, is an AI text generator that can help inspire creativity in writing and presentation creation. It provides ideas, helps with brainstorming, and supports lesson planning, making it a useful, time-saving tool for educators. (Magic Write is not available for student accounts through Canva EDU unless the district turns on the feature.) Canva Text to Image generates an image based on the description you enter, while Magic Edit and Magic Erase offer AI assistance for editing photos. Magic Design is one of my favorite tools for getting a jumpstart on visually engaging presentations, lessons, or even videos for class. You simply enter five or more words that describe what you hope to create, and let Magic Design do its magic. Using Magic Switch, teachers can transform a design into a document, email, presentation, or other format. Canva also has a translation feature capable of more than 130 languages, which promotes accessibility for ELL students and communicating with families.

✦ **Conker** enables you to create standards-aligned quizzes and formative assessments with more than ten question types. It also offers a library of examples that illustrate ways to use the tool. Teachers can search the content bank or add their own topic and have questions created. For example, you could have students read an article and respond to questions about it that were created by Conker. Or, you could save valuable time by prompting Conker to create a quick assessment for you. Conker also provides a read-aloud feature for students.

✦ **Curipod** enables teachers to create interactive lessons or "curipods" in minutes using AI. Starting with a prompt and selecting a grade level or content area, for example, a lesson with content and activities will be generated. Teachers can also import a PowerPoint or a PDF. Students can explore various topics, and the AI functionality helps generate customized lessons tailored to their learning needs. You simply type in a topic, and Curipod generates a ready-to-run lesson. Lessons can include slides and activities such as drawing, answering open-ended questions as shown in **Figure 3.2**, polls, and having students submit words that will be used to create a word cloud, which can spark more discussion. (Try the code CURIRACHELLE to gain access for creating additional lessons.)

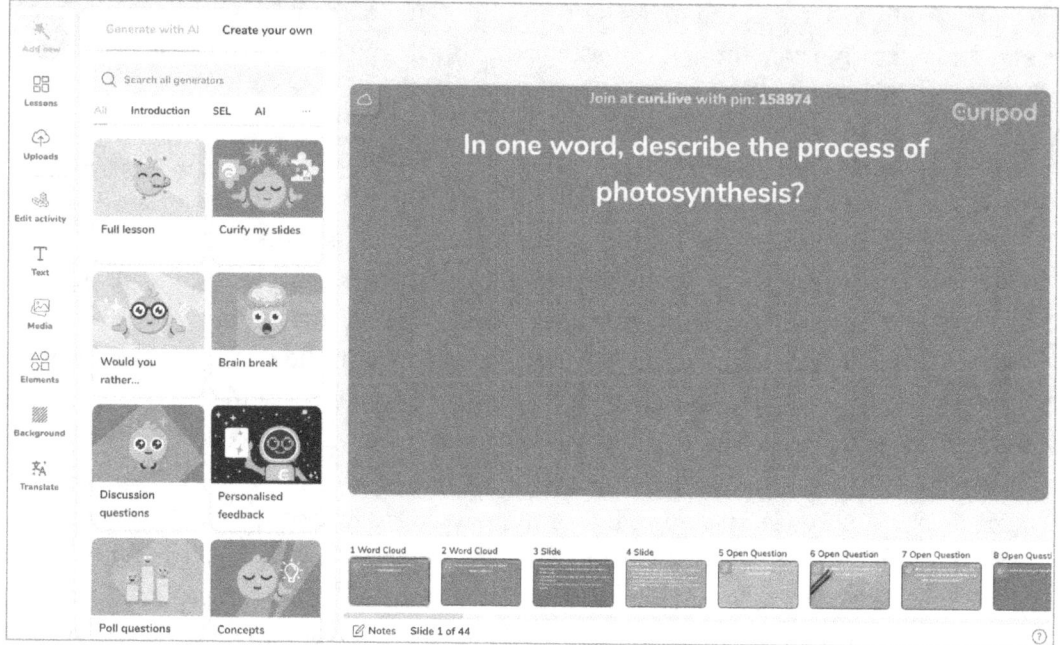

FIGURE 3.2
One of the slides with an activity generated within Curipod. You can see the layout of how to create the lesson.

✦ **Diffit** enables teachers to obtain leveled resources for students across multiple grade levels and for any type of content or lesson. Useful for grades K–12, this AI-powered platform can break down text into chunks, differentiate them for multiple reading levels, and summarize text. Teachers can quickly generate resources such as discussion activities, vocabulary activities, assessments, and more. You can even enter the URL for an article or a video, choose a grade level, and specify a language, and then let Diffit generate resources for you such as documents, Google Forms documents, and presentations (**Figures 3.3** and **3.4**). It also suggests an image to add to the content.

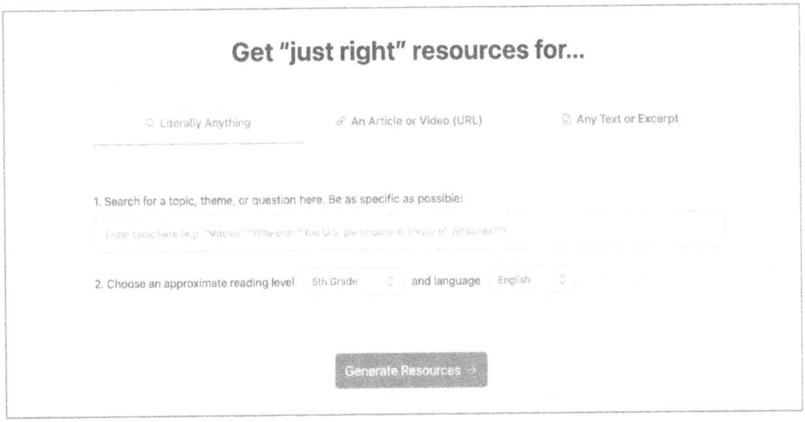

FIGURE 3.3
Diffit can create resources on any topic for the grade level and in the language you specify.

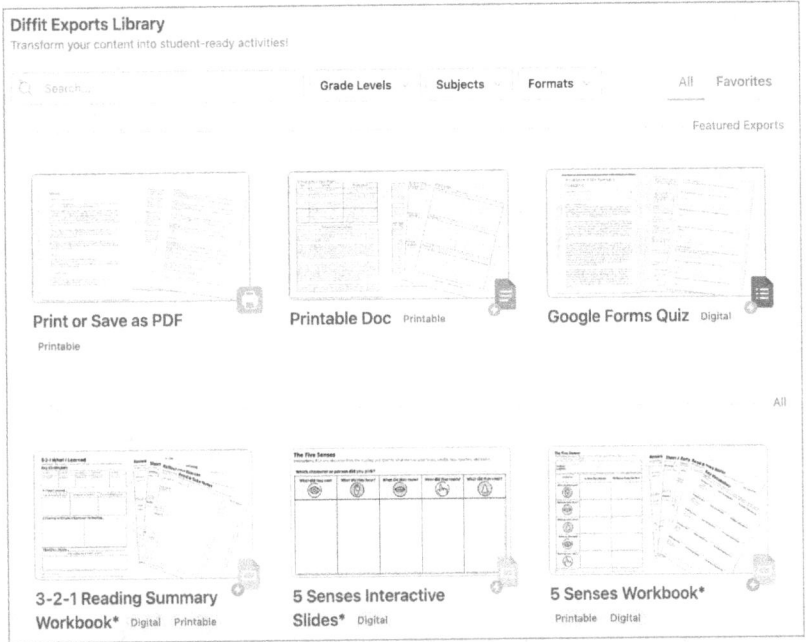

FIGURE 3.4
You can export your Diffit-generated resource in multiple formats.

✦ **Eduaide.Ai** is a platform for AI-assisted lesson planning to help teachers create high-quality instructional materials in a more effective, efficient, and timely manner. You interact with large language models (LLMs) to generate lessons and activities based on the topics and grade levels you specify. Some of the tools available from Eduaide.Ai include a Content Generator, Teaching Assistant, Feedback Bot, Free-form Chat, and an Assessment Builder (**Figure 3.5**). You can choose from more than 100 types of resources, such as class activities, email templates, quizzes, virtual labs, lesson plans, and various types of questions. Language translation is also available.

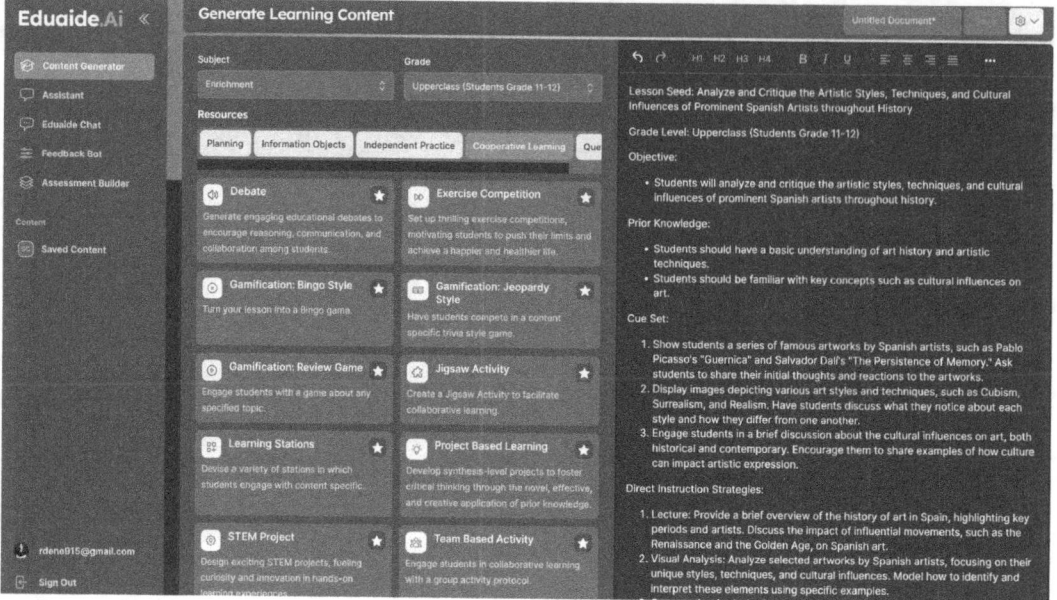

FIGURE 3.5

In Eduaide, you select the type of resource to create, and the generated results appear in a workspace on the right. You can edit and save the lesson, as well as create games, activities, assessments, and more that connect to the topic.

✦ **Formative** is a versatile platform for teachers to create assessments, interactive lessons, quick check-ins, and more. Through AI, it can auto-generate questions based on standards, as well as provide auto-generated hints for students as they work. It uses algorithms to analyze student responses and provide personalized feedback to students.

✦ **Grammarly** is a writing assistant that you can add to your Chrome extensions to help with any type of writing. It will highlight text that has spelling, grammar, or punctuation errors, as well as make recommendations for improved sentence structure. You can also use it in emails, which I find quite helpful!

✦ **MagicSchool AI** provides a variety of time-saving resources for educators. You can write lesson plans, differentiate instruction, create assessments, write IEPs, communicate with families, write newsletters, and more **(Figure 3.6)**. Use generators to create science activities, reading quizzes, and even teacher jokes. Finding resources is easy through the search option or filtering by task type, such as planning, content, questions, or student support. MagicSchool's AI chatbot, Raina, can be used to ask questions, summarize text, and more **(Figure 3.7)**. And recently launched MagicSchool for Students (MagicStudent) helps build AI literacy skills for students.

FIGURE 3.6
The categories of resources that can be generated by MagicSchool AI

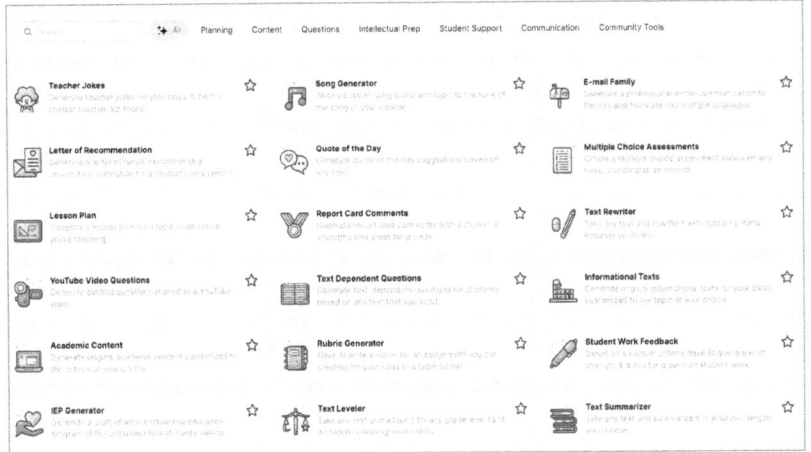

FIGURE 3.7
You can use the Raina chatbot as a teaching assistant for brainstorming ideas and completing a variety of tasks based on the prompt provided.

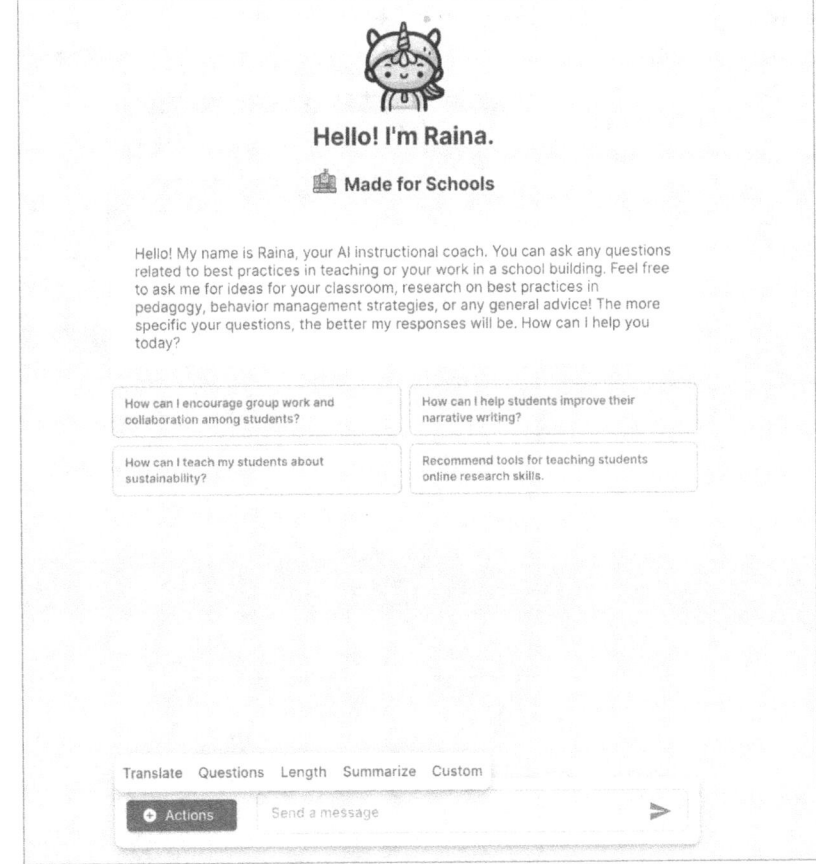

- **Parlay Genie** creates age-appropriate discussion prompts for your students. You enter a discussion topic or a link to a video or article, select the number of questions you'd like, specify your students' grade level, and click Generate Prompt. Parlay Genie then generates questions about the subject or source material for your students to review and discuss.

- **Passed.AI** is a Google Chrome extension that detects AI-generated text and more. Designed to help educators ensure academic integrity, it can scan a Google Docs document to provide not only an AI score but also a full document audit. The audit report (**Figure 3.8**) dives deep into the history of the document: who contributed to it and when, the number of changes made to the document, the time spent on the document, the number of large text insertions, what and when changes were made, and more. The Replay tool lets you watch a reconstruction of the document's creation from start to finish.

FIGURE 3.8
A Passed.AI audit report shows the contributors and provides insight into students' work done in the document.

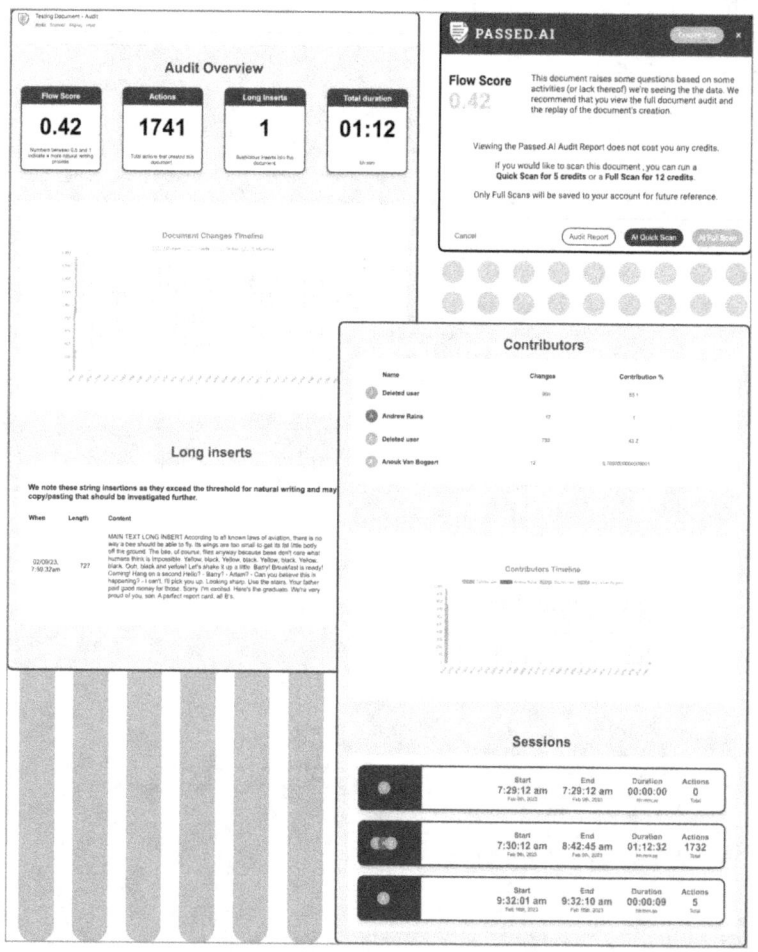

- **QuestionWell** helps you create formative assessments. You can upload or input a reading, and then the AI will analyze it and generate objectives, multiple choice questions that focus on specific content, essential questions, learning outcomes, or content area standards. Plus, you can export the questions to game-based learning tools such as Blooket, Gimkit, Kahoot!, and Quizizz, or an LMS such as Canvas or Schoology.

- **Quizizz** uses AI to automatically generate quizzes from documents (PDF, PPT, or DOC files), videos, or web pages. Quizizz analyzes the content of the source you provide or link to, then creates a list of questions (**Figure 3.9**). You can also use it to enhance quizzes (either those you find in its Content Library or the ones you create) by checking grammar, adjusting question difficulty, adding in real-world context, translating languages, and more.

FIGURE 3.9
The options available within Quizizz for using the AI-enhanced features to generate quizzes

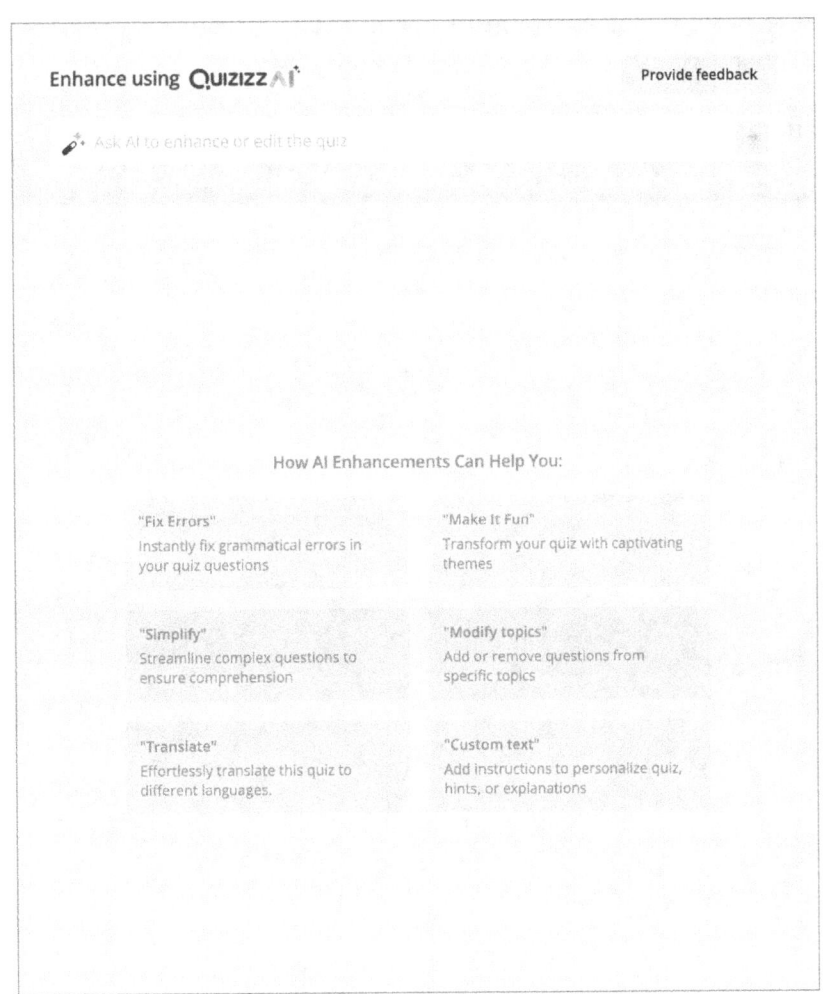

✦ **SchoolAI** offers three different features to help educators and students: Coteacher, Spaces, and Mission Control. Coteacher can assist with a variety of tasks; you can make a specific request or select from one of the available "chat actions." In **Figure 3.10**, you can see some of the tasks that Coteacher can help with, such as generating course outlines, an IEP, lesson plans, newsletters, quizzes, a class syllabus, worksheets, and more. Coteacher also has specific AI assistants including AI in Education Coach, Common Core Expert, Digital Literacy Coach, and Research Assistant, plus more on the way. Spaces are AI-powered student experiences that can be used with grades K through 12. Teachers can set up a Space by leveraging the AI and providing customized instructions or selecting from SchoolAI's library of content, which is organized by subject. In Spaces, students engage in a chat focused on the specific content, and the chat will adjust based on the student's level of understanding to offer a more personalized learning experience (**Figure 3.11**). Through Mission Control, teachers can also see the chat activity and insights that are provided.

FIGURE 3.10
SchoolAI's Coteacher can create a variety of resources.

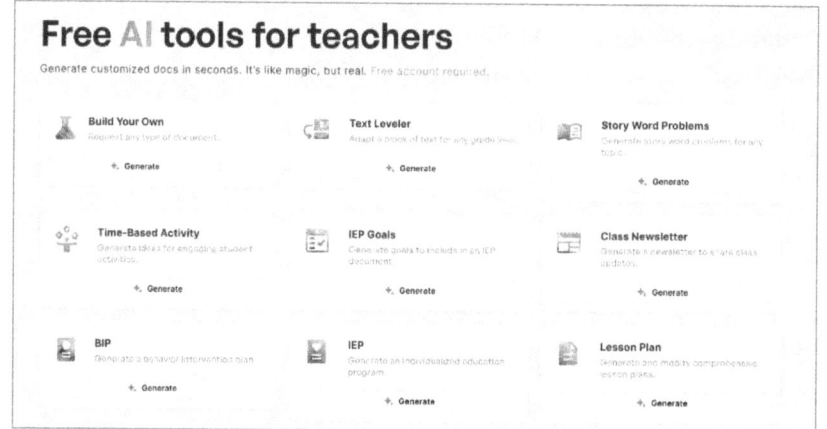

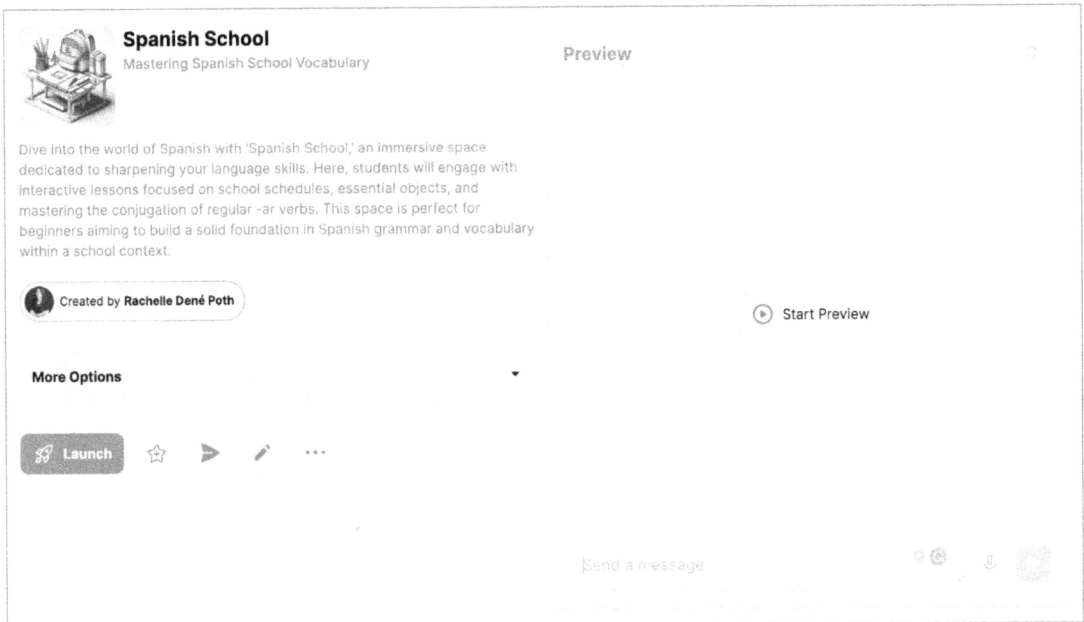

FIGURE 3.11
I used SchoolAI to create a Spanish Café Space and a Photosynthesis Space, each of which engages students with chatbots in conversations related to the specific prompt and content that is provided.

Don't be afraid to explore these tools. As educators, we must guide our students and ready them for the future by equipping them with knowledge and skills to navigate the world of AI effectively and ethically. To be prepared, we need to practice with and research the tools ourselves.

By leveraging the right tools with balance, we can increase the time available for our students, providing them with a world full of opportunities, personalized to their needs and instantly available to them. AI tools can also help us better target our instructional practices for each student by giving us access to customized resources and other materials that track progress and learning patterns.

You can find additional resources for teachers in Appendix B or by scanning the QR code at the end of this chapter.

How to Begin with AI Tools

Diving into the ocean of available AI-powered tools can feel daunting. First and foremost, remember to always think about your purpose when looking for a tool to enhance your classroom. Using technology for technology's sake or because it's the latest hot trend is never the best path. Ask yourself some questions, such as what is the tool going to help you provide for your students, what are the benefits for them, and does it offer an experience that is otherwise unavailable for them? The more confident you are in your reasons *why* you are going to use a specific tool and how you believe that it will improve students' learning experiences and their outcomes, the more easily you can share those reasons and benefits with your students, which I feel is important to do.

▶▶▶▶ Take a look at your classroom and consider where you might see the biggest benefits of using AI. Be sure to consider your many tasks besides teaching; these can take up a lot of time that would be better spent working with students or engaging in professional learning. AI-powered tools can help you reclaim and redirect that time. Ask yourself:

✦ How am I spending my class time?

✦ What are some of my time-consuming clerical tasks each day?

- Can AI help me do some tasks faster so I have more time with my students?

- How do I provide differentiation for students?

- Will my students benefit from having access to AI tools rather than a traditional lecture or other activity?

- Are there digital tools that enable students to drive their learning while also receiving feedback to grow on?

- What are the concerns with the tools that I'm going to use in my classroom?

- Have I reviewed guidelines, policies, and privacy statements?

Thinking about my own classroom, some of the most time-consuming tasks are creating and reviewing assessments, locating appropriate supplemental activities for differentiation, offering more engaging and self-driven learning experiences, being available for students whenever they have questions, and providing the exact practice they need when they need it. For you, perhaps the challenge is grading assessments, or maybe communicating and collaborating with students or with families eats your time (think emails and newsletters). AI-powered tools can facilitate all this and more.

Once you have identified an area to focus on, look for a tool with features to help. For example, a tool with language translation capabilities could help promote inclusivity and greater accessibility for all learners, as well as assist with communicating essential information to families with different language needs.

When considering tools, take precautions to make sure that the product is in compliance with relevant laws, such as COPPA (Children's Online Privacy and Protection Act) and FERPA (Family Educational Rights and Privacy Act), as well as school guidelines. Check all of the safety information to make sure that it is suitable for your students and that no data is taken from the students when using it—and if it is, how it is used. Here are some questions to consider:

- Are the tools being used in compliance with all safety and security protocols?

- What are the benefits of using this technology?

- Are we adhering to the age requirements for student use of these tools?

- Is data being collected from students and educators?

- Do we understand what is being done with any data that is collected?

▶▶▶ When you've decided on a tool to try, become familiar with it. Create an account, check the privacy settings, and look to make sure it is in compliance with COPPA and FERPA. While it's tempting to jump straight to test-driving the features, it is essential to first review the appropriateness and policies of each tool to prioritize student safety and privacy.

Once you have verified that it adheres to your school's policies, test it out with one activity—create a quick quiz, write an email, or do some other small task to start. Before I introduced ChatGPT to my students, for example, I spent hours on a Saturday night exploring and testing the program. I gave it prompts that I used in my Spanish courses, asked it to write stories using the vocabulary and verb tenses that I provided, and gave it multiple discussion questions based on the content that I was teaching in my courses, just to see how quickly and accurately it would respond. I assigned it the role of a Spanish teacher and gave it prompts to generate project ideas, quizzes, lesson plans, and rubrics.

Evaluate how it performed in your tests (I had to adjust some of what ChatGPT generated), and consider whether another available tool provides less or more. If your tool exceeds other options, continue working with it and definitely dive into creating more content that will help save time and improve your workflow.

Finally, share what you are exploring with your colleagues so that we all can continue to learn and grow together.

Key Takeaways

As students interact with AI through the digital tools in the classroom, they develop skills in technology use and also understand where they are in their learning journey through the AI-powered tools they use. (*ISTE Standard 1.1.c Empowered Learner*)

Opportunities to interact with AI also help students better understand how to evaluate and use the information they obtain, which, in turn, helps them develop essential media literacy skills. (*ISTE Standard 1.3.b Knowledge Constructor*)

Educators, too, must continue to build new skills and apply them in their own learning, and this requires educators to stay current with technology. (*ISTE Standard 2.1.c Learner*)

By implementing new tools in the classroom, you will develop confidence in your professional practice and will be able to share ideas and model best practices for colleagues and students. (*ISTE Standard 2.2.c Leader*)

Through the use of AI-powered tools, educators can explore new ways to provide instruction while also creating opportunities for students to build digital literacy skills. (*ISTE Standard 2.3.b Citizen*)

tinyurl.com/ykt7c8z9

Exploring new tools and ways to leverage AI in the classroom is a great way to learn with and from students. (*ISTE Standard 2.4.b Collaborator*)

Keep exploring beyond these pages: scan the QR code for a list of resources and tools to try.

Questions for Reflection and Discussion

This chapter offered an overview of the benefits and changes AI tools bring to the classroom, as well as some specific ideas for time-saving tools to help you create valuable instructional materials for students and be more efficient and productive with other classroom tasks. After reading this chapter, take a moment to reflect on what you've learned and consider:

✦ How does the use of AI-powered technologies in education align with the goals of student-centered learning and personalized instruction?

✦ In what ways can you collaborate with AI systems to maximize their potential in enhancing the learning experience for all students?

✦ How might you use AI as a tool to promote higher-order thinking skills and creativity among students?

✦ What are some potential challenges you may encounter when implementing AI in your teaching practice, and how can you address them?

Share your ideas with me on X (formerly Twitter) @Rdene915 or post a message on LinkedIn.

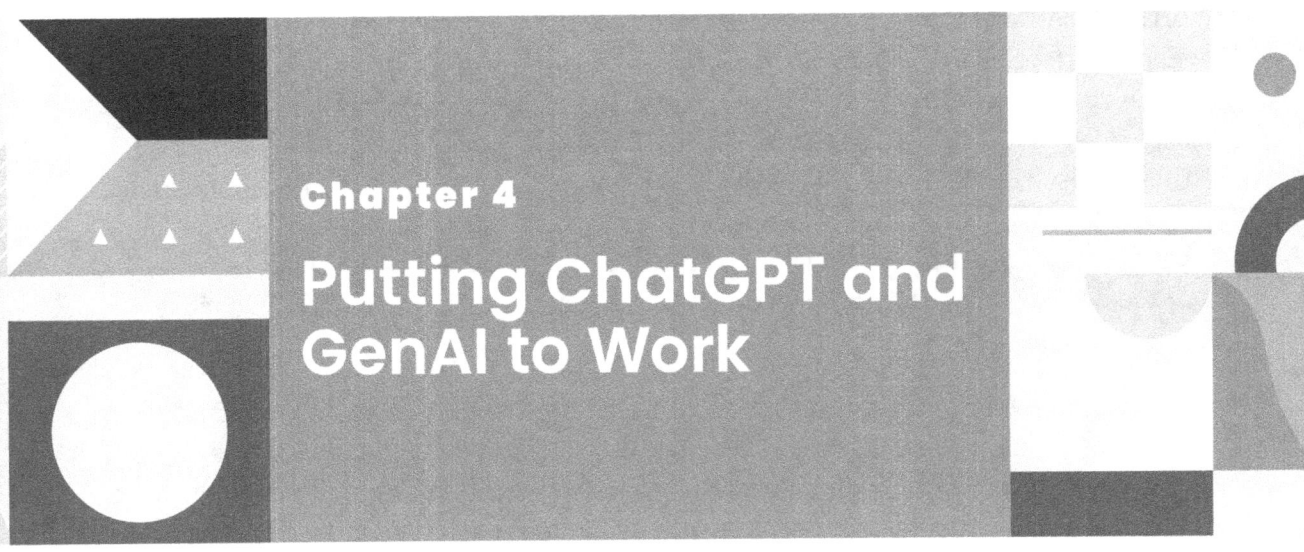

Chapter 4

Putting ChatGPT and GenAI to Work

The content of this chapter aligns with the following standards and indicators:

ISTE Student Standards

1.1.d Empowered Learner

1.3.d Knowledge Constructor

1.4.d Innovative Designer

1.5.d Computational Thinker

ISTE Educator Standards

2.1.a Learner

2.2.c Leader

2.3.b, 2.3.c Citizen

2.4.b Collaborator

WITH RESPONSIBLE USE and an understanding of the potential for bias and inaccuracies in AI responses, generative AI (GenAI) tools can transform student learning and enhance your workflow—just ask your colleagues. In a 2023 Study.com survey, teachers responded that they believed ChatGPT could help students build such skills as critical thinking (39%), problem-solving (38%), and data-analysis (32%). More than 25% mentioned ChatGPT aiding with editing skills, digital literacy, language learning, reading comprehension, and creativity. Although 43% of the respondents believed that the generative AI tool would make their jobs more difficult, the majority believed that it would make their lives easier.

Generative AI tools, such as ChatGPT, Google Gemini, Claude 3, Microsoft Copilot, Perplexity, and YouChat, can streamline many of your time-consuming tasks, freeing you to work directly with your students or fellow educators instead. Whether you need to outline a lesson plan; create project ideas; try a new approach to a frequently taught topic; design a project that includes standards, relevant objectives, activities, and pacing; write a letter of recommendation or grant proposal; or draft an email asking for parent volunteers, give ChatGPT a prompt. It will generate content and ideas to help you. It's that simple—or it should be.

Nothing in life is perfect, however, and even AI can go askew sometimes, which is why crafting an effective prompt is a vital skill for you and your students. The more specifically you can guide an AI-powered tool with your prompts, the more focused its responses will be to your needs and the less adjusting the results will require. In this chapter, we'll discuss how to write prompts to get the best responses from GenAI tools, as well as look at ways to help students use generative AI tools at all grade levels.

Prompt Engineering

Prompt engineering is an essential skill that will help you and your students obtain the type of output that you are looking for from ChatGPT and similar tools. First and foremost, make a prompt clear, concise, and specific to what you want. Asking an open-ended question, such as *What is AI?*, will give you a lengthy and potentially very technical response, depending on your prompt's topic. Asking ChatGPT to limit its response to a given number of words or to provide specific examples will help you narrow its focus. A better way to create a prompt is to assign ChatGPT a role, include a specific grade level, and ask ChatGPT to explain a concept to students at that grade level. For example, use the prompt *You are a fifth-grade teacher and you want to explain AI to your students. Provide a definition and three examples of AI that students would understand. Limit your response to 300 words.* A prompt like this is specific and concise and will leverage the full potential of ChatGPT.

▶▶▶ Work with your students to develop their prompt engineering skills: Have conversations about why prompt wording matters and how to phrase a strong prompt. With older students, you can test prompts in class and discuss their results, if ChatGPT or other GenAI tools are available. Phrasing a prompt to produce the needed output requires that students think at higher levels and focus on specifics rather than general questions. You can push students to build critical thinking skills by working on creating prompts and analyzing the output from ChatGPT and other similar tools. How do they differ and what do students notice?

BETTER PROMPT ENGINEERING

Prompt engineering matters, but how can you improve your prompts? Be clear, concise, and specific.

Consider a couple prompt makeovers:

Weak: *What is artificial intelligence?*

Stronger: *In 300 words, what is AI and can you provide at least three examples of how AI is used?*

Strongest: *In 100 words, explain what AI is, and provide an example for educators and one that is used in daily life.*

Weak: *How does AI work?*

Stronger: *Your role is a [content/grade level] classroom teacher. Explain how AI works so that a fifth grader would understand it, and provide at least 3 examples and 3 follow-up questions for them to discuss.*

These are just a couple examples, but they can be good starting points to have students evaluate. If possible, test out the responses that ChatGPT or another LLM generates.

At the same time, you can teach students to assess the reliability of the information produced by their prompts (both strong and weak ones). Was the generated response accurate and relevant, or was the AI tool hallucinating? In AI terms, *hallucinations* are inaccurate results (sometimes wildly so) that an algorithm generates and presents as fact. They happen because AI models are trained to predict words that match your prompt, but they do not have logic or reasoning to be able to identify inconsistencies in facts. When I prompted ChatGPT to write my bio, for example, the output read very well and convincingly, however, it was not fully based on facts (**Figure 4.1**). It hallucinated a PhD for me as well as a professorship—neither of which I had at that time. Similarly, prompting an AI image generator with *create a picture of a moose in a pickup truck* might result in an image with a moose body embedded in the hood of the truck rather than the animal sitting in the driver's seat or truck bed as you expected.

FIGURE 4.1
When I prompted ChatGPT to write a 300-word bio about me, I received this convincing but creatively inaccurate response.

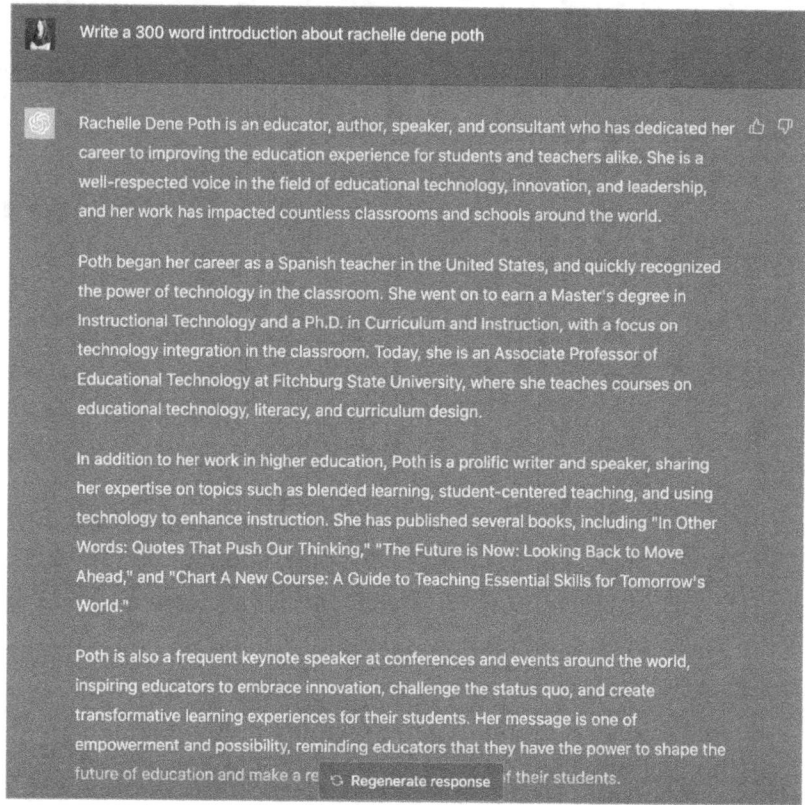

> Write a 300 word introduction about rachelle dene poth
>
> Rachelle Dene Poth is an educator, author, speaker, and consultant who has dedicated her career to improving the education experience for students and teachers alike. She is a well-respected voice in the field of educational technology, innovation, and leadership, and her work has impacted countless classrooms and schools around the world.
>
> Poth began her career as a Spanish teacher in the United States, and quickly recognized the power of technology in the classroom. She went on to earn a Master's degree in Instructional Technology and a Ph.D. in Curriculum and Instruction, with a focus on technology integration in the classroom. Today, she is an Associate Professor of Educational Technology at Fitchburg State University, where she teaches courses on educational technology, literacy, and curriculum design.
>
> In addition to her work in higher education, Poth is a prolific writer and speaker, sharing her expertise on topics such as blended learning, student-centered teaching, and using technology to enhance instruction. She has published several books, including "In Other Words: Quotes That Push Our Thinking," "The Future is Now: Looking Back to Move Ahead," and "Chart A New Course: A Guide to Teaching Essential Skills for Tomorrow's World."
>
> Poth is also a frequent keynote speaker at conferences and events around the world, inspiring educators to embrace innovation, challenge the status quo, and create transformative learning experiences for their students. Her message is one of empowerment and possibility, reminding educators that they have the power to shape the future of education and make a re ⟳ Regenerate response f their students.

Sharing ineffective prompts and hallucinations creates an opportunity to highlight the importance of focusing on evaluating resources and also to discuss why there might be errors. If you have a subscription to ChatGPT Plus, you may encounter this phenomenon less because GPT-4, on which it's based, has been shown to have significantly lower rates of hallucinations compared with prior versions of GPT (Wodecki, 2023).

By Dr. Michael Harvey, Physics teacher, Marlborough Boys College, Blenheim, New Zealand

I am a physics teacher who wants to teach my students about kinematics, especially projectile motion. I decide to use Chat GPT-4, a generative AI tool that can create decision trees and flow-charts based on natural language prompts. I ask students to write a prompt using the PREP model, which stands for Prompt, Role, Explicit, and Parameters. The students come up with this prompt:

You are a level 2 NCEA student studying the level 2 mechanical systems achievement standard. Create a decision tree for the use of the four kinematic equations on motion. The decision tree must find each of the unknown variables, if you have the other variables.

I type the prompt into Bing AI chat in the creative mode and show the students the result. The tool generates a decision tree that matches the NZ curriculum and helps the students choose which equation to use for different situations. The students are impressed by how Chat GPT-4 can understand their prompt and create a useful diagram.

Next, I ask the students to create a flowchart based on the decision tree. I explain that a flowchart is another way of showing the steps of a process or algorithm. The students use Chat GPT-4 again to generate a flowchart that follows the same logic as the decision tree. They also see an example of how to use the flowchart to solve kinematic problems.

The lesson concludes by asking the students to reflect on how Chat GPT-4 can help them learn physics concepts and skills. I also encourage them to explore other applications of generative AI in education and beyond.

Practice Your Prompts

The best way to improve your prompts is with practice. Think about some of the tasks that you ask students to do, type those into ChatGPT, and then evaluate the responses you receive. Are they accurate and relevant? Do they provide the information you look for from students? If not, revise the prompt you entered to get it closer to your intended result.

Another great way to practice prompts is to ask ChatGPT to generate a project overview, complete with a rubric and description of the required format and the specific tasks that students have to complete (**Figure 4.2**). You could even ask it to incorporate specific ISTE Student Standards or content area standards, to provide some discussion questions, or to add activities for enrichment. Go a step further and prompt it to generate a timeline with estimated deadlines to help students learn how to pace their work.

FIGURE 4.2
An example of a clear
prompt with a role
assigned to ChatGPT
and the output
generated

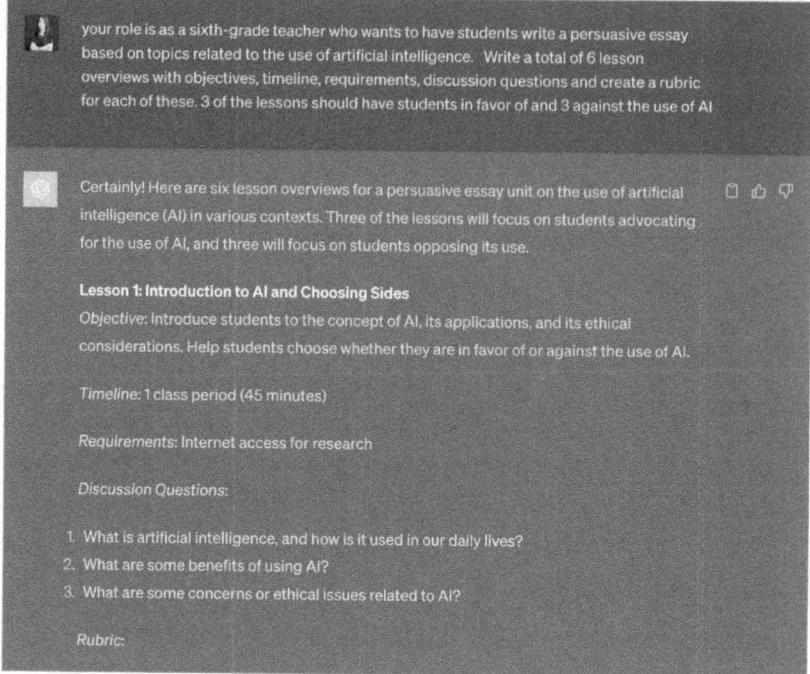

While having what usually takes you hours appear in minutes is exciting, be sure to check the results. Is the information accurate? Is the project like something that you would create and then share with your students? If it meets your standards, you can then add your own authentic and personalized content that best meets your students' needs and interests. If you're consistently dissatisfied with the accuracy of the free version's results, ChatGPT Plus might be worth its subscription price. I have this version and it is well worth it. The GPT-4 model that underlies it is more powerful and provides greater accuracy. Planning a good prompt takes a lot less time than planning a full lesson, giving you time to spend working with students and looking for additional resources or ideas for your classroom.

Similarly, you could use ChatGPT as a time-saver to help you structure your content when writing a syllabus for a new class. If you have an outline of a course description, enter it into ChatGPT and prompt it to add more details, write a longer introduction, or include relevant standards, for example. Using it for this purpose simply enhances what you already have and casts AI as your assistant.

▶▶▶▶ Need more quick ideas for prompt practice? Ask ChatGPT to create a fun story to hook students into a lesson, or to write word problems using a theme or in the tone of a character for a math class. Ask it to personify a character from history and describe an event or engage in a conversation with students. These are only a few of the many ways that you can use ChatGPT not only to create and extend learning but also teach students about the power of generative AI tools.

Twenty Prompts to Save You Time

Here are twenty prompt ideas you can try that can help with the creation of class materials, communications, and more. The prompts will work for any grade level with ChatGPT, Google Gemini, Microsoft Copilot, Claude 3, Perplexity, and other generative AI tools.

✦ **Class intro:** *Write an introduction to [class] in the theme of [you pick] or the voice/narrative style of [you pick].*

✦ **Course syllabus:** *Create a syllabus for [course]. The course is [length] and the main topics are [list topics].* Or have it revise or provide feedback for a syllabus you have.

✦ **Build relationships:** *Provide 10 activities or fun icebreakers for getting to know students in the [grade level].*

✦ **Differentiation and scaffolding:** *For teaching about [topic], provide 10 options for differentiating instruction for students with varying learning needs.* Scaffold: *Create a guide with step-by-step instructions for students about [topic/lesson] and include pacing.* Be sure to include length of class periods or a specific time for the activities.

✦ **Updates and newsletters:** *Write an email for parents that shares information about [class topic].* Newsletter: *Write a class newsletter that includes...* Add to the prompt specific dates, events, and key points that you want the newsletter to include.

✦ **Activity and game creation:** *Create 5 activities for my students about [topic].* Games: *Create a game about [topic] and for [grade level] that accommodates [number of players].* You can specify whether the responses should include technology or be hands-on activities and games.

✦ **Creative lesson ideas:** *Provide 5 lesson plan ideas for teaching [topic] to [grade] students.* You also can include a reference to standards or any specific requirements that you have, such as class period length and activity types.

✦ **Lesson hook:** *Create a hook to a lesson on [topic] in the voice of [a famous character or some other fun theme].*

✦ **Lesson planning:** *Write a lesson plan for [grade level] on [topic] with standards, learning objectives, class activities, project ideas, and a short assessment.* You can also ask it to create enrichment and lesson extension activities.

✦ **Projects:** *Generate 10 ideas for student projects on [topic] that include assessments, reflection questions, and potential options for tools.* You can provide parameters such as project type, standards, and length of project, as well.

✦ **Quiz creation:** *Create a [number of questions] quiz that includes open-ended, true/false, and multiple-choice questions. Also include an answer key and generate sample open-ended responses.*

✦ **Teaching strategies:** *Provide a list of 5 teaching strategies that can be used to boost student engagement and that differentiate for student ability levels in a lesson on [topic].*

✦ **Reading comprehension:** Paste an article into ChatGPT, then prompt *Generate 10 questions [true/false, multiple choice, discussion].* You could also request follow-up activities.

✦ **Presentation on new topic:** *Create an outline for a 10-slide presentation that includes key points, timeline, and discussion questions on [topic] for [grade level].*

✦ **Worksheet:** *Create a worksheet on [topic] for a [grade level/course]. Include open-ended, matching, and a variety of question types and tasks.*

✦ **Rubric creation:** *Create a rubric for a project on [topic] with point breakdowns for each category and descriptions.* You can also provide the categories or point values (**Figure 4.3**).

FIGURE 4.3
A simple rubric generated by ChatGPT with criteria and point values

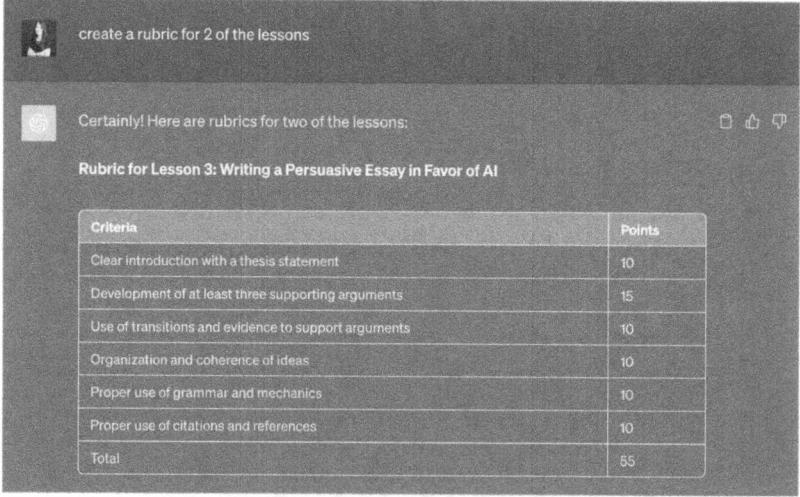

create a rubric for 2 of the lessons

Certainly! Here are rubrics for two of the lessons:

Rubric for Lesson 3: Writing a Persuasive Essay in Favor of AI

Criteria	Points
Clear introduction with a thesis statement	10
Development of at least three supporting arguments	15
Use of transitions and evidence to support arguments	10
Organization and coherence of ideas	10
Proper use of grammar and mechanics	10
Proper use of citations and references	10
Total	55

- **Feedback generation:** *Generate 3–5 responses to provide student feedback based on [this response].* You would need to paste in the student's response. Remember to remove any personally identifiable information.

- **Personal assistance:** *Generate questions to help me better understand [topic].* Or, *Provide alternate ways of presenting [topic] to students.*

- **Saving time:** *Summarize [paste in an article or something that you have written, or with GPT-4 Turbo, upload a document] and generate [number and type of] questions.*

- **Creative and off-beat lesson ideas:** I try to make learning easier by using mnemonics or music. Ideas: *Write a song about [topic] in [style of] that will teach students about [topic].* Or, *You are [famous person being studied] and you are engaging in a conversation or debate with [another famous person].* Select people from varying backgrounds, eras, fields of work, and more.

When you create an effective prompt, save it! I've collected a list of hundreds of prompts, and it's still growing. You can also find a huge variety of prompt lists online in blogs or in books. Explore the prompts shared by TeacherMade, the Teaching Channel, and ClassPoint for some content-specific prompts as well as prompts for clerical tasks. Find what works for you and then generate your own!

EDUCATOR'S PERSPECTIVE: AN ENGINEERING CHALLENGE FOR CHATGPT

By Jennifer Bond, MS Design Tech teacher and Innovative Teaching and Learning Specialist, Michigan

I introduced ChatGPT to my middle school Design Tech students, and I gave them a demo of some of the common ways people could use ChatGPT, including writing song lyrics, creating essays, forming a weekly menu for family dinners, as well as taking suggestions from students in the class. Then I created a prompt that asked ChatGPT to create an engineering challenge for a class of middle schoolers that incorporated specific materials (which I had ready to go on a table in the classroom). I also set a time-limit of 20 minutes, and I asked it to be themed patriotic, as we completed the challenge on September 11. ChatGPT generated somewhat different challenges each class period ranging from patriotic towers to bridges and parade floats. In addition, we asked ChatGPT to create a rubric so that the students could self-assess their design when they were done with it.

As with all new technologies, we need to make sure that we explore the benefits and concerns. Don't be afraid to explore these tools because as educators, we need to be prepared to guide our students and help them understand the technologies that may become an even bigger part of their future.

Generative AI: Beyond Text Creation

As we discussed in Chapter 1, *generative AI* refers to a class of AI models and systems that use algorithms to learn patterns from existing data, and then apply those patterns to generate new content in a process called *generative modeling*. So far, we've focused on text, but generative AI tools can also create images, audio, video, and more. There are many opportunities to test out creativity and have fun exploring and learning about the capabilities of generative AI. Beyond text-based uses we've talked about, GenAI can help expand your creativity and that of your students in many areas and ways, such as:

✦ ▶▶▶▶ **Audio generation:** GenAI tools can create new audio content, such as music, podcasts, and even audiobooks—all in realistic-sounding voices. One of my favorites is Speechify (**studio.speechify.com**). As you can see in **Figure 4.4**, you type in text, select the type of voice and emotion you want, and then hit play. It is a fun activity to try! Ask students if they can tell the difference between human and AI-generated speech, and if so, how? Have them listen to and analyze the speech patterns of recordings, looking for any unique traits or ways to tell that it is AI-generated.

FIGURE 4.4
Designing a fun voice to read text is a great way to engage students in a lesson while learning about AI.

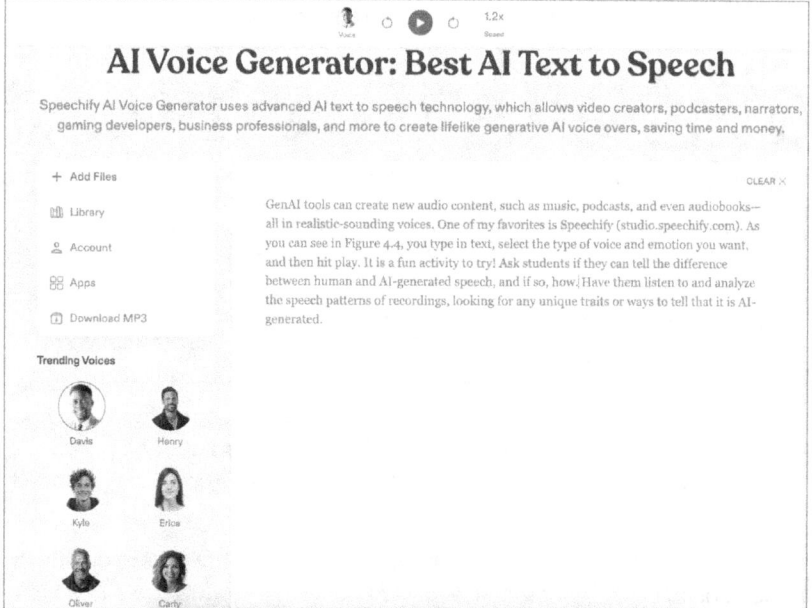

✦ **Image analysis:** You can upload an image to ChatGPT Plus (the GPT-4-based paid version), and prompt the platform to analyze it. In response, ChatGPT Plus will describe as much as it can about the possible location and time of day depicted, as well as detail why it came to its conclusions.

✦ ▶▶▶▶ **Image editing:** GenAI can create new images, artwork, and visual designs. Depending on the tool, it can analyze an image and create a new image using *style transfer*, which means applying the artistic style of one image to another. For example, students could choose a painter, upload a photo, and have the AI tool generate their image in the painter's style. What type of mix is created when selfie meets Sergeant? Using this activity in any class can be an easy way to bring in some AI lessons. Generative Fill features can add content to extend an image, remove objects and fill in "behind" them, and more. For tools with these options, try Canva and even ChatGPT Plus.

✦ ▶▶▶▶ **Image generation:** With AI-powered tools, such as DALL•E, Craiyon, and others, you can create realistic or fantastical images in the style of photographs, paintings, cartoons, specific artists, and more from text prompts or drawings (**Figure 4.5**). DALL•E 3 is now available through ChatGPT Plus, and Canva also recently added a text-to-image generator. A fun activity is to use Craiyon or another tool to write a silly prompt with a few unrelated objects, characters, and themes and see what the software generates (**Figure 4.6**). You can then use this as a hook for a lesson or a prompt, having students write or discuss what they see. Some students hesitate in drawing, and this spark of inspiration might be just what they need. Other tools like Adobe Firefly and Microsoft Designer enable you to type in a text prompt and have a work of art or a 3D avatar generated. Microsoft Designer functions similarly to Mad Libs: fill in the blank with random words and descriptors, and it generates a 3D character!

FIGURE 4.5
The prompt provided and the results generated by DALL•E. The four images can spark fun conversations.

FIGURE 4.6
The prompt provided
and image generated
by Craiyon. As a fun
lesson hook, have stu-
dents describe it.

✦ **Music:** AI tools can create songs and even entire musical compositions. For students to retain content, they need authentic and meaningful ways to practice. Creating mnemonics or short songs that are catchy can be a great way for students to remember the content. Sometimes it is tough to be creative, but by inputting the text and prompting ChatGPT or other generative AI, you can create something fun for learning. Another tool to explore is Stable Audio, which enables you to create a song or sound based on text prompts. With it, students can make custom backgrounds for videos or podcasts, giving them the chance to be the creators!

✦ **Video generation:** With GenAI tools, you can create new video content, such as movies, TV shows, and commercials, including realistic videos of people and objects. Educators can generate an AI avatar with voiceovers in more than 120 languages using a tool such as Synthesia or D-ID. Both enable you to create a video from a photo, choose from one of their avatars, or generate a cartoon avatar. Plus, OpenAI is working on Sora, a tool that creates videos from text prompts, but at this writing no release date has been announced. Diving in and creating with the tools and modeling their use for students is important. Students can make multimedia presentations to explore AI. It builds content skills but is also a great way to collaborate, create, and innovate. It can be used in different grade levels and content areas and help with sparking curiosity and creativity in learning.

Generative AI has shown incredible benefits for creativity and innovation, but it also presents challenges related to ethical considerations, bias, and the potential for producing misleading or harmful content. Some are questioning copyright issues related to the images that are being used for training AI, as well. In early 2023, Getty Images took Stability AI, the creator of Stable Diffusion (an image generation tool), to court in the U.K., claiming Stability AI used Getty's copyrighted image library for training without consent; Getty also filed a similar copyright infringement lawsuit in the United States (David, 2023). In September of 2023, the Authors Guild filed a lawsuit against OpenAI, alleging that ChatGPT had been trained on their work without their consent or knowledge, thus violating copyright (Wiggers, 2023). In contrast, Adobe has pledged a "creators first" approach to ethically source training data for its AI tools (including compensation and credit mechanisms for contributors) and to combat bias through rigorous oversight (Adobe, 2024a, 2024b). The U.S. Copyright Office is monitoring this emerging area and is asking for input on the issue; however, there have not yet been clearly defined court decisions to provide insight (Wiggers, 2023).

▶▶▶▶ What are your thoughts, and what do your students think? Bring these issues into your classroom. Start a discussion or a debate with students that focuses on whether tech companies should be able to use images or text from other sources as training data, without the consent of the creator/owner. For example, should images that are found online become part of training data so that generative AI tools have access to more in order to have more capabilities? Students can also research to find additional examples and share with classmates.

Ideas for Using Generative AI in the Classroom

As technology continues to advance, the capabilities of generative AI are expected to expand, impacting various industries and aspects of our lives. This is why we need to create opportunities for students in all grades and content areas to explore the capabilities of this technology, while reinforcing responsible usage themes and digital literacy. As educators, it is our responsibility to prepare students for their future by equipping them with knowledge and skills to navigate the world of AI effectively and ethically. To do this, we have to create and explore with them. Consider your assignments and activities carefully. Ask yourself: Can what you're asking for be accomplished quickly by ChatGPT or another generative AI tool without substantive student engagement? If so, rethink the activity. Just as if something you ask is "Google-able," then you're not asking the right question! To help you get started, the sections that follow offer activity suggestions, prompts, and ideas for a variety of content areas across all grade levels.

✦ Activities for Elementary or Middle School

You can use GenAI tools not only to teach students about the power of this technology but also to enhance their learning experience and supplement typical course materials. The following ideas work as activities for students to explore on their own or as a team. Note, also, that you can use ChatGPT (as suggested) or a similar tool. As a fun class activity, involve students in selecting which tool to use for these activities.

+ **Language arts class:** To spark young students' creativity, prompt ChatGPT to generate a story beginning or characters based on some related keywords, then ask students to continue the story. This is a fun and engaging way to encourage students to convey their ideas and learning, as well as exercise their imagination. You could provide ChatGPT with some of a reading that you have provided for students and then upload the document or PDF (if you have access to a paid version). Ask it to generate a new story, create discussion questions, or take on the role of one of the characters and write a narrative about the character for students to read.

+ **Storytelling:** Ask students to suggest an animal, color, random object, setting, and any other item they can think of, and then prompt ChatGPT to generate a short story incorporating those suggestions. (You could use the vocabulary specific to your lesson.) Once the story is ready, ask students to read it and discuss how well the AI tool generated it. To extend the lesson, break the class into groups and ask students to continue the story.

  ▪ For older students, use ChatGPT to generate a few stories and share those with students to read in class and discuss. Students can learn to evaluate the writing style of AI and practice differentiating between AI- and human-written text. As students analyze the story, they develop their critical thinking skills.

- Have students work together with ChatGPT to create collaborative stories. They can take turns adding sentences and see how the AI contributes to the narrative as "co-author." This activity introduces students to GenAI's capabilities and possible limitations while enhancing student creativity and teamwork.

- **Character interviews:** Have students choose a character from a story they are reading or one they have written themselves and prepare interview questions to ask the character. Enter parts of the story into the prompt along with instructions for ChatGPT to portray the character while students conduct an interview. An activity like this will help students think deeply about the chosen character's motivations, traits, and development, enhancing their comprehension and analytical skills. It will also help connect them to the story in authentic, meaningful ways.

- **Spelling and grammar practice:** Use ChatGPT to create an interactive spelling activity or grammar exercises based on specific content or focus areas for your students. For instance, you could prompt ChatGPT to generate a certain number of sentences with errors, and then ask students to identify and correct these mistakes. Or, have students create sentences, and then explore how AI can assist in proofreading and editing their written work. Some questions to consider are whether using it for this purpose was efficient and whether the output from ChatGPT was error-free. Ask students if they can tell whether the sentences were created by AI or not. Why or why not? An extension would be to use Grammarly to explore how AI analyzes the writing and provides recommendations, and then compare.

- **History and social studies:** Use ChatGPT to create an interview between two historical figures being studied, or select a famous event in history and ask ChatGPT to predict how that event might change if it occurred today or in another time period. If ChatGPT or a similar tool is available in the classroom, involve students in creating additional questions to engage in a conversation. If it's not, create the prompt and generate the output to then share with the class.

- **Math:** Have ChatGPT act as the quiz creator or personal tutor for math quizzes or flashcard-style exercises. Students can ask ChatGPT to generate random math questions within a specific topic or to create questions at a certain difficulty level to help students build their skills. This gamifies math practice and helps students reinforce their mathematical concepts while (hopefully) having fun. You can also provide an incorrect solution to problems and test if ChatGPT catches it and explains the correct answer. As a follow-up, ask it to then generate additional practice problems for students to work through. (Be careful, though; ChatGPT has made multiple mistakes when I have used it for math.)

⊼ Activities for Middle School and High School

To bring learning to life and make it more meaningful, it is important to show older students the capability of AI technologies in their everyday lives. We want them to value their learning experience—not just consume content but also create. With quick adjustments, you can use the ideas from the previous section with higher-level students. In addition, try the following.

✦ **Science:** Ask ChatGPT or other generative AI tool to provide prompts with which students can simulate virtual science experiments. To get started, prompt ChatGPT to design different scenarios for students to explore. For instance, if students are studying photosynthesis, ask it to create examples for students to process as they build their knowledge. For a course on chemistry or physics, prompt it to create a challenge or experiment (or several) based on a relevant topic such as chemical reactions or design and engineering challenges, and ask students to explain how they would work through the experiment, or design an experiment based on the parameters. For example, ChatGPT might respond, "Simulate the trajectory of a projectile launched at varying angles and velocities. How do these parameters affect height, range, and time of flight?" These ideas would help spark curiosity and creativity in learning and also give students the chance to reflect on what they learned in the process. Another idea is to assign ChatGPT the role of a *[content area]* educator, teaching about *[topic]*, and ask it to generate scenarios or discussion topics for students to consider or projects for them to design, focused on a particular concept.

✦ **Social studies:** Few tools can bring history to life and increase engagement like AI. For example, students can use Hello History to select a persona from a variety of historical figures and engage in a virtual conversation with it. Similarly, you could set up a historical role-play activity where students interact or debate with AI-generated historical figures—either as modern-day students or playing a role contemporary with their selected historical persona—to gain insights into different perspectives on events of historical significance. Students can ask questions, prompt ChatGPT with a specific role or character from history, and have a chat to see what it comes up with. With these ideas and more, students can learn about specific people, events, or time periods in history.

✦ **World languages:** Students sometimes are a bit hesitant to speak in front of their classmates, especially when they're building language skills. Instead, get students involved in simulated conversations in the target language with a chatbot, ChatGPT, or other generative AI tool. By removing the fear of judgmental peers, chatbot conversations will help students develop skill, comfort, and confidence in speaking, which with practice will transfer over into the real classroom space.

Activities for High School

For a long time, I thought of myself as *just* a Spanish teacher, and as such I could not address topics like AI in my classroom. I've since realized that we *all* have an obligation to help our students understand these technologies as they emerge—no matter what our content specialty. In some manner, *all* students will encounter AI in their future lives, not only those whose goal is to code the algorithms that power it. So why not help students learn about AI from as many perspectives as possible while they are in our classrooms? There are many ways we can tweak our lessons to highlight AI and its benefits. Here are just a few examples that you can use or adapt to your specific content area to make them relevant, authentic, and meaningful for your students.

+ **Arts and design:** Prompt ChatGPT to compare art styles or to predict how two artists or designers might create something new that merges their styles. After the response is received, students can then use the information to make their own designs. Students could create a prompt that focuses on specific artists or art styles and ask ChatGPT to create a new style that merges those specific artists. Then task students to use their knowledge of art styles with the information from ChatGPT to create a new work of art and then discuss how they created it. The use of generative AI tools such as Adobe Firefly is also beneficial for exploring art and using it as a model to have students design in.

+ **Computer science:** Use ChatGPT to write lines of code with a specific number of errors for students to debug and explain why the code will not work. Students can explain what is wrong with the algorithm and then work individually or together to debug it. Another idea is to have students write their own lines of code and ask ChatGPT to review and/or debug the lines of code that they have written, pointing out errors and alternative solutions. Of course, adhering to age requirements with these tools is essential. Depending on students' ages, they could share the code with their teacher, who can then complete the ChatGPT task. An activity like this can facilitate conversations between students about coding and how to identify errors, as well as lead to greater understanding of the limitations and benefits of using AI-powered technologies.

- **Culinary arts:** Use AI to generate recipes from a random list of food items. Students can evaluate the recipe that it creates and discuss the healthiness of the recipe, potential taste, and preparation involved, and perhaps then create their own similar recipes or come up with a new idea for a restaurant. Students could also use ChatGPT to ask for suggestions for food presentation or complementary dishes for a meal. A fun activity might also be to use some generative AI tools to design ads or menus for a restaurant that students are creating.

- **Economics:** Use AI to simulate stock market scenarios to help students understand supply-and-demand dynamics and economic decision-making. Create some prompts to guide a discussion, or prompt ChatGPT to come up with interview questions and scenarios for students to apply their learning. For example, you could use a prompt like this: *Provide a list of 5 teaching strategies that can be used to boost engagement and that help educators provide differentiation for student ability levels in a lesson on [topic from the course].*

- **Literature:** For more advanced courses and readings, provide excerpts from the reading to ChatGPT (or similar tool), and ask it to generate discussion questions on the passage or to generate prompts for students to complete a literary analysis. Depending on the types of prompts that are generated, this activity could stimulate critical thinking and class discussions—whether on the topic of the reading or to evaluate the AI output. It is also fun to task an AI tool with a certain theme or character to engage students more in learning. A student could prompt, for example: *So, Ahab, what is with your white whale obsession?* As a Spanish teacher, I might use it to interview Don Quixote and have students provide questions to ask. Use AI as a way to learn more about the setting of a novel by asking for a more detailed explanation or to write an adjusted story by changing the time period or setting of the story and then compare.

- **Music:** There is a ton of potential for exploring generative AI when it comes to music. Using the Human vs AI Test from Tidio (**tidio.com/blog/ai-test**), have students decide whether the music files were created by human or AI. Or, shift students to being creators and have them explore using AI to generate a music composition. They can experiment with different sounds and melodies, gaining insights into music theory and composition. Provide a prompt that asks the AI tool to merge the style of one artist with the style of another to write a song; students can see what it comes up with and then have a discussion about it. Some tools, such as MagicSchool AI, offer a song generator that can be really fun to test out— especially with a good mix of words and themes.

Time-saving Ideas for Teachers

Chapter 3 introduced twelve of my favorite time-saving tools but still only scratched the surface. AI-powered tools can help you with editing, convert audio to text so you can speak your revisions rather than type, create presentations and other instructional materials for use in the classroom, and more. Sometimes you just need generative AI to create a basic design for you; then you can focus on the best content to add to meet your students' needs. The following list offers more suggestions for time-saving ways to use AI and tools to try. (Remember, of course, to always review the AI-generated content for appropriateness and accuracy.)

+ **Assessment tools:** In Chapter 3, I shared examples of how easy it is to generate a variety of assessments and lessons or presentations—and there are still more tools to help you! In my language classroom, for example, I want students to speak and write in the language, but sometimes doing this in front of others is uncomfortable for them. With a tool like Snorkl, I can create prompts, tell the AI what I want students to do, and opt to have AI-generated feedback provided. Students can even download their recordings for use in creating a podcast or a multimedia presentation to represent their learning. Give it a try as a way to better understand what your students are thinking and to be able to provide them with timely feedback.

+ **Research assistance:** I have started to think of ChatGPT, Google Gemini, Microsoft Bing, Claude 3, Perplexity, Copilot, YouChat, and other commonly used chatbots as research assistants. Based on GPT-4 (the top AI model as of this writing), Perplexity can respond to speech or text prompts to research whatever you need, for example. The answers it provides include links to various articles that it referenced, as well as images. You can also create your own AI profile so that it will provide you with more personalized answers. (When adding the app to my phone, it provided information about data safety and a reminder that the app may share data types with third parties and collect the data but that it is encrypted and you can request that your data be deleted.)

  - ▶▶▶ If you're interested in creating a personal chatbot trained on your own data, you can try out Zapier and Dante AI. For example, I created a chatbot for my website with Dante AI; I uploaded links and documents, and it generated a chatbot that can provide responses based on my content. When someone visits my site now, they can more easily find information or research topics with the help of my chatbot.

+ ▶▶▶ **Lesson hooks:** Using generative AI tools to create images can be a great way to spark interest and hook students into the lesson. Adobe Firefly, DALL•E 3, Midjourney, and Craiyon are at the top of my list and the ones that I have used most frequently. Based on your prompt—either a simple or a detailed text description—each tool generates one or more images. There are text effects, and you can use many of the other tools available. In my language classroom, I often ask students to give me some prompts for DALL•E based on what we're learning and then have my students describe the resulting image in Spanish. It's a fun way to keep learning going and also learn about AI. You can use generated images (from your prompts or students') to engage students in discussion, prompt them to write a description, talk about what they see, and more.

✦ **Lesson materials:** Brisk Teaching, Curipod, Diffit, Eduaide, fobizz AI, LessonPlans. AI, MagicSchool AI, SchoolAI, Schemely, and Twee are just a few of the many tools for designing lesson plans, educational resources, and instructional materials. Brisk is a free Google Chrome extension that enables educators to provide feedback, inspect student writing, develop educational materials, and level and translate texts to meet their students' needs without leaving their current workflow. With Twee, for example, English teachers can generate dialogues and stories, create different question types, and even provide a URL for a YouTube video to have questions created. With Diffit, you can select from a variety of resources such as Google documents, presentations, Frayer model, and more for students to engage with the content. It also provides options for adjusting the Lexile level for students, and you can edit all of the content that has been generated. A favorite in my class has been SchoolAI, which has some great options for students to engage in a chat with famous people such as Alan Turing, Frida Kahlo, George Washington, Harriet Tubman, and more. Or, you can create a "Space" and design the type of chat for students to engage in (**Figure 4.7**).

FIGURE 4.7
SchoolAI offers topics for educators and students to explore through chat, or you can create your own Spaces.

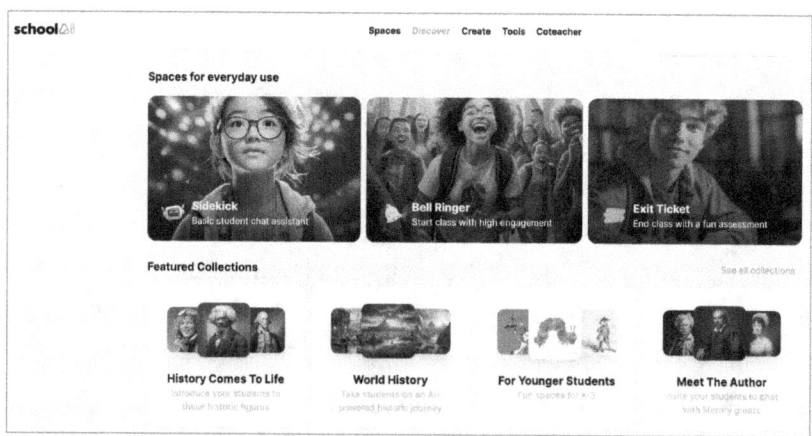

CHAPTER 4: PUTTING CHATGPT AND GENAI TO WORK

- In addition to these tools (many of which are free), I have used ChatGPT to generate ideas and to evaluate and potentially revise content I wrote, simply to test its reliability. For example, you can provide it with one of your prior lesson plans and prompt it to include additional activities, project ideas, and assessments. These tools also include language translation capabilities, templates, and many resources to help you more quickly create more interactive and engaging lessons. We started with Curipod, and my students loved it. I noticed a boost in student engagement, and it was way more interactive for them.

- With Schemely, you can create a lesson plan or even a whole course. For lesson plans, you can prompt Schemely to include a slide presentation, Quizlet flashcards, a Kahoot! quiz, a YouTube video link, a variety of activities, assessments, and ideas for differentiation. Like EduaideAI, Schemely was built by educators who understand the needs of teachers and students; developers of both platforms continue to seek feedback to improve what they provide.

✦ **Presentations:** If you struggle with making presentations, generative AI can help you generate visually engaging and interactive presentations beyond what you can do with traditional tools. At the same time, they enable you to explore and learn about the potential of AI and share that with your students or colleagues. Canva, Tome, Slidesgo, and SlidesPilot are in my regular lineup. For comparison, I created the same presentation using each one to see how their results differed in design and in content, as well as if one was more accurate than the others. Also, I looked for any negatives, such as generating images that represented only one gender or ethnicity, completely unrelated images, inappropriate images for the target age group, or hallucinations. I was curious to see how my prompt was analyzed and used to generate my presentation (**Figure 4.8**). Each had a unique style ranging from a basic presentation to a more professional one (Canva and SlidesPilot), or very visually engaging graphics to coincide with the topic (Tome).

FIGURE 4.8
An example of my presentation created using Tome, for a case study assignment

Be sure to check out the resources list in Appendix B for additional ideas for exploring AI and the many generative AI tools available. Scan the QR code at the end of the chapter to access a Wakelet-based collection with a list of tools to explore. The list will continue to be updated as tools become available or new features are added over time.

Study Aids for Students to Explore

Whether you are continuing your own learning by taking courses, are working on advanced degrees, or would like to offer your students some new study aids, the following AI tools can help. Be sure, however, to always verify the sites used and age requirements before recommending them to your students.

✦ **Chatbots as virtual tutors:** TutorAI will generate a personalized lesson in response to a student's prompt.

✦ **Research assistants and editors:** PowerNotes can help students, educators, and other professionals gather resources and even provide citations. Similarly, Grammarly can help writers with their grammar and spelling, even making suggestions to improve writing style.

- **Career prep resources:** Interviews by AI creates a mock interview based on the job description that you upload and will provide real-time feedback. If students aren't that far along in their career search, CareerDekho is a great resource to help them learn about career paths and find a career of interest.

- **Note-taking assistants:** I enjoy using AudioPen to record my thoughts as I am reflecting on something that I have read. It then generates a cleaner text version, with grammar edits included. It can streamline the process of note-taking and capture ideas more quickly, leaving more time for focused writing or project work.

- **Content-creation tools:** Depending on the age of your students, using some of the previously mentioned text-to-image or text-to-video tools is a great option for enhancing the learning experience and also promoting accessibility. For example, Luma AI released a Discord bot called Genie, a text-to-3D AI tool. With Genie, users enter a text command and will then receive four 3D models that also have a link to download the object or simply view it. For boosting creativity, students can bring their ideas to life even without 3D modeling experience. The tool is also a benefit for anyone interested in game development.

And that list is just a start—it can feel overwhelming. In 2010 Apple trademarked its slogan *There's an app for that*, but now we can say, "There's AI for that." As of June 2024, in fact, there are more than 12,500 apps for 15,000 tasks and 4,800 jobs, available for use on the site theresanaiforthat.com. After you explore the tools in this chapter, check out the site to discover (and try) the transformative technologies that are being developed. Search AI content detection tools, avatar makers, chatbots, image generators, online courses, presentation tools, video generators, website builders, and more.

Key Takeaways

In this chapter, we took a dive into the resources available for learning about and creating with generative AI and how to use ChatGPT. It is essential that students understand emerging technologies and how they work and to become creators. (*ISTE Standards 1.1.d Empowered Learner, 1.3.d Knowledge Constructor, 1.4.d Innovative Designer, 1.5.d Computational Thinker*)

For educators, it's essential to develop an understanding of these emerging technologies and prepare not only to provide learning experiences but also collaborate and co-learn with students. Staying current with research and mentoring students on ethical and responsible use of these tools is critical. (*ISTE Standards 2.1.a Learner, 2.2.c Leader, 2.3.c Citizen, 2.4.b Collaborator*)

Educators must provide opportunities for students to explore and create. To do so requires ongoing professional learning and the sharing of that learning with colleagues and students. (*ISTE Standards 2.1.a Learner, 2.2.c Leader*)

Educators also need to actively review the tools and model the ethical and responsible use of these tools in the classroom. (*ISTE Standards 2.3.b and 2.3.c Citizen*)

Together, educators and students can discover new ways to leverage the tools available. (*ISTE Standard 2.4.b Collaborator*)

Scan the QR code to check for new tools; as I find tools and evaluate them for classroom use, I'll add them to the list.

tinyurl.com/ykt7c8z9

Questions for Reflection and Discussion

There are many options to explore for creating a variety of supplemental learning materials, and we can leverage the available tools to spark curiosity, meet students' individual needs and interests, and best prepare them for the future. After reading this chapter, take a moment to reflect on what you've learned.

✦ Reflect on a specific AI technology or use that you find interesting. How might you incorporate it into your teaching to spark curiosity and promote critical thinking among your students?

✦ What are some projects or activities that can encourage students to explore the boundaries and possibilities of AI?

✦ Imagine you need to create a project that showcases the capabilities of one of the AI types covered in this chapter. What would you create, and how could it benefit society or enhance learning?

✦ How can understanding the distinctions between AI types empower educators and students to make informed decisions about the AI tools they use?

Share your ideas with me on X (formerly Twitter) @Rdene915 or post a message on LinkedIn.

Chapter 5

Fostering Creators and Innovators with AI

The content of this chapter aligns with the following standards and indicators:

ISTE Student Standards

1.1.d Empowered Learner

1.3.d Knowledge Constructor

1.4.d Innovative Designer

1.5.d Computational Thinker

ISTE Educator Standards

2.1.c Learner

2.2.c Leader

2.3.b, 2.3.c Citizen

2.4.b Collaborator

SUCCESSFULLY INTEGRATING artificial intelligence into your classroom is all about achieving balance. While AI can certainly enhance the learning experience for students, it cannot replace the human connection that needs to exist in our classrooms. We want to provide students with opportunities to explore the many AI tools available and to be independent in their learning experiences. At the same time, we need to find balance and avoid overreliance on AI capabilities. Students need ongoing interaction with teachers and their peers to develop essential interpersonal skills as well as skills in critical thinking, creativity, and emotional intelligence. Even when students explore on their own, they still need teachers to provide them with feedback to help them grow. A teacher can provide personalized feedback that takes into account each student's unique strengths and weaknesses—something that AI cannot replicate. Yes, chatbots can act as virtual tutors for students, but their feedback is not the same as the authentic, meaningful, and personalized feedback provided by a human teacher who truly knows each student.

Similarly, although we want students to explore and create with AI tools, we must continue to offer them traditional learning activities that enable them to interact with their classmates. It is important that they develop essential skills that come through interpersonal connections that happen in the classroom and the real conversations that happen between classmates. Again, we have to find the right balance.

But, how? We've talked about AI's benefits; discussed the need to be vigilant about minimizing bias, protecting data privacy, and using AI to supplement, not replace, learned skills; and even dug into a few tools you can use. Still, we've yet to discuss what may be your biggest questions: How do I put this all together in *my* classroom? How do I balance it all? This chapter will help you.

Learn Together

One way to better fit AI tools to your purpose is to embrace the technology and test-drive some of the tools yourself. Artificial intelligence is something that should and can be taught at all grade levels, no matter what your content specialty. Before deciding you don't see the value in a method or tool or that it has no applicability in your work, take time to explore thoroughly. In our quickly changing world, investigating ways to bring AI into your classroom is essential.

▶▶▶▶ Show students that you may not be an expert, but you are taking a chance with something new. You are learning about AI, and you want to learn with them. Sharing your experiences with students encourages them to explore on their own and share what *they're* learning. Students will build meaningful skills, and you will gain a better understanding of how AI can benefit them—and the times when AI can't compete with innately human qualities and the importance of human collaboration and the building of relationships.

▶▶▶▶ When we are intentional about modeling responsible use, students can learn how to use AI for good. Involve students in coming up with problems that need to be solved and task them to create their own AI tool to solve the problems. Engage them in discussions about how we can be proactive to avoid being replaced by AI in the future of work. By giving all students the opportunity to understand, explore, and design AI, we will foster innovation and provide experiences through which they will develop the competencies needed for the changes that AI might bring.

While it can feel uncomfortable to not know the answer to a question that students may ask, we simply need to know enough to get our students started. Bringing AI into our classrooms and getting the conversation started are the most important steps. We don't have to be the experts. It's important that we learn from our students and give them a chance to become the creators and to thrive in a way that meets their specific interests and needs. When this occurs, it leads to more authentic and meaningful learning.

Learn from Mistakes

As you've seen in previous chapters, many resources are available to make getting started with artificial intelligence easier than ever for educators. We can now provide learning activities for students, even on a short-term basis, without spending a lot of money on specialized programs and equipment. In fact, even AI's drawbacks can become a learning opportunity.

I can't say it enough: To ensure responsible use by students, we have to focus on ethical considerations and accuracy when using generative AI tools. A concern is that these tools will lead to a decrease in critical thinking and creativity in students. I believe the opposite, however. When used properly, with a clear purpose, they can actually promote the development of some of these skills—in particular, critical thinking. Knowing how to evaluate and fact check is vital, because students and educators alike need to be able to determine the accuracy of the information obtained through generative AI tools.

▶▶▶ When we share content with students that has been generated by ChatGPT, for example, we can further involve students in extended learning opportunities. Ask students to analyze the generated information for accuracy and credibility. Has it been properly cited? Ask them to scrutinize generated images: Do they contain any irregularities? Are students able to evaluate the image to see patterns that help to distinguish between human-made and AI-generated? These are just a few examples of ways that we can teach students and guide them to develop their analytical and critical thinking skills. These activities will help them to learn to distinguish between real and fake news and between credible and unreliable resources.

Fortunately, more companies are adding disclaimers or reminders to their sites stating there is a chance that the information generated by the AI may not be accurate. Look closely at websites with your students; read the fine print to check if there are any concerns about privacy and data being shared.

⤧ Activity: Google Search Lab Experiments

In the fall of 2023, I noticed that Google Search had changed. Google Search Labs was experimenting with a new feature that generated AI responses to inquiries as well as returning the usual results. Initially, it was in the form of a "short response paragraph" that I could expand to see greater detail or ask a follow-up question. A note warned about the reliability of the information provided because the feature was experimental, and I did not always receive the most accurate or current information. I could, however, click a Thumbs-Up or Thumbs-Down icon to provide feedback on each generated response to help train the AI model, called SGE.

To turn on this feature in Google Chrome or the Google app, make sure you're logged into your Google account and then click the Search Labs icon (it looks like a beaker). On the next tab, you can toggle on SGE for all searches to receive an AI-generated overview as well as the usual search results. There is also an option to turn on SGE while browsing; do so, and SGE will scan the resource you're browsing and summarize its key points to help find what you're looking for faster. (iPhone users can toggle between traditional Google searches and the AI-generated overview now too.)

You can use Google's SGE search feature as an activity with your class: Have students evaluate the generated content, and engage them in a discussion about the benefits and negatives of receiving summarized information rather than lists of resources. They can work together to brainstorm ideas and to do some fact checking. The activity reinforces the fact that not everything they find on the internet is accurate, which will help them to learn how to distinguish between fake news or images and build the essential skills that help them to analyze, evaluate, and process information from any source. Be sure to encourage students to ask questions, test out their own searches, check the accuracy of the generated content, and share their findings with classmates. Not only is this a good way to explore the capabilities of AI, but it is also beneficial for collaboration and building essential critical thinking skills.

EDUCATOR'S PERSPECTIVE: BOOSTING CREATIVITY WITH AI

By Laura Steinbrink, High school English teacher, Missouri

As an English teacher for Waynesville High School in Missouri, it has been challenging for me to consider the uses of AI with students. Using it personally as a teacher has been quite the revelation too. My biggest hurdle has been reconciling the potential benefits with the potential risks of the AI doing the thinking and creating for either myself or my students. I am a big proponent of using tools to support and enhance learning, but I have been wrestling with the idea of having such a tool that could do the work, the thinking, and the creating instead of the student. How should we utilize that power for students?

Here are a few ways that I see it helping students:

- **Brainstorming:** AI can quickly generate ideas to help students with projects, writing, and any information needed to get them started.

- **Project-based learning (PBL)/Genius hour:** When experts in a certain field of work are not available to students, AI can provide students with the information needed to fill gaps in their knowledge or thinking. This works hand-in-hand with using AI for brainstorming as well. It can guide students through the intricacies of the chosen field for the PBL or genius hour.

- **Writing:** While I prefer that students do their own writing, they are often unsure of how to start. The blinking cursor on a blank page has intimidated or thwarted many student and adult authors. AI can generate the start of their assignment so that they can easily continue or begin their own path through the narrative, prose, research, etc. It can also serve as a writing coach, and I am all in favor of it helping students improve their writing as well.

- **Creative writing:** Students can use AI to generate a beginning of a story and complete it themselves, the middle of a story and create the beginning and end themselves, or the end of a story and create the beginning and middle. AI could help students create their own "choose your own path" story too.

Putting It Together: The First Lesson and Beyond

Whether directed by school leadership or motivated by your own research (or even inspired by ideas from this book), there comes a day when you have to present your first AI lesson to your class. Now what? With so much information that's so rapidly changing, organizing it all can be daunting. Keep it simple: a good lesson can grow from one good question, hook, conversation, or story.

For example, each year when I first teach my students (or other educators) about AI, I start the same way I started this book: I ask what they think of when they hear the term *artificial intelligence*. The responses can lead the conversation in different directions, such as analyzing how the technology generally works or what a tool or app does that involves AI. After the initial discussion, I always play an introductory video to get students started thinking about AI and spark more conversations in class. During the first few class periods, I share some short videos that demonstrate different types of AI (Appendix B lists some ideas for these). Some of the videos give an overview of what AI is and how it works, others show chatbots and how they are programmed, and still others show humanoids and advanced AI technologies. I really like the video series available from the CrashCourse AI YouTube channel. I use this with my eighth graders, and it is a great resource for older students. For younger students, I recommend the video *What Is AI? Artificial Intelligence Facts for Kids* from Hey! Guess What. After showing the video, I ask students what they notice or how they think that AI is involved in what they saw. We then exchange ideas about how we are using AI or where we see AI being used in everyday life. Discussing ways in which AI is making an impact can lead to some additional ideas from students and even spark some new ideas.

After some initial videos and open discussions, we then start to explore various websites and tools over a period of about eight weeks. A discussion always follows our activities, and I often demonstrate tools that fall under the generative AI category to show students how quickly it creates an image or a lesson. Everything we do is followed up by a conversation about the pros and the cons (such as how generative AI tools should not be a total replacement for the creativity that comes from humans), and then we try to be creative and think about what other ways we could use a specific tool or how AI could benefit a person in various aspects of life and work. Showing them some examples of where AI is used every day that they may not realize also sparks some curiosity and excitement for learning. We dive into some resources such as videos to see AI in action in various areas of life and work and we try to dream big about the possibilities that AI could provide.

Amidst all these big dreams, however, I am sure to ask students if they have any ideas about potential *negative* impacts of AI technology. For example, how do they feel about the use of facial recognition software in public? Do they feel it violates a person's privacy? How would they feel if they found their pictures online without their permission? I then ask their opinions on the use of facial recognition in different areas of work, such as law enforcement or education, and see if their responses change.

Sometimes I demonstrate a specific tool for students; other times I keep the demo brief and give students time to dive in on their own. Occasionally, students hesitate because they feel that they won't be able to complete a task or they won't understand a concept, but that's when sharing our own stories comes into play. The majority of us are not experts when it comes to artificial intelligence; I wasn't at first, and I'm still learning now.

Each year that I have taught my STEAM: What's Next in Emerging Tech class or presented a session focused on AI, I always start with this same approach. Each experience provides an opportunity for me to learn more and for students or educators to feel more comfortable getting started with AI in the classroom. It also builds excitement for something new. Once we have a basic understanding, then we begin looking at some uses of AI and find resources to interact with AI.

That said, beyond the introductory lesson, I don't always follow the exact same plan or use the same tools. I like to be flexible with topics and activities throughout the year, adapting my AI curriculum based on the students I'm working with, their interests, and the knowledge that they bring with them to our classroom. Also, the tools are constantly changing, bringing with them many new and exciting opportunities for exploring AI. Sometimes our students already know a lot more than we may give them credit for. Each year, my students bring a lot of interesting insights to the classroom, and it is a great way to learn with and from them. What's important is to find resources that give all students the opportunity to learn about artificial intelligence and its capabilities. Provide space for students to explore on their own and find something that piques their interest. Doing so enables us to be a facilitator and, maybe more importantly, a co-learner with our students, which is highly impactful.

◥ RECAP: DAY 1 PLAN FOR TEACHING ABOUT AI

So, you might still wonder, "How do *I* actually start teaching about AI?" Here's an example for that first day or even first few days, depending on how your class discussion goes.

1. Begin class with a quick brainstorm about what students think of when they hear the words *artificial intelligence*.

2. Spend time asking students to respond and give examples. Follow up by asking why they think that the technology they mentioned is AI or how it uses AI.

3. Show the six-minute video, *What Is AI?* (**youtu.be/mJeNghZXtMo**).

4. Following the video, ask students for their thoughts/questions about AI. Did anything change about their understanding of it?

5. Provide students with clearer definitions for *artificial intelligence, machine learning*, and *natural language processing*. Share some examples and ask students to provide some additional examples. Depending on students' age, you can have them do a quick internet scavenger hunt to find examples of each of these.

6. As a class, brainstorm examples of the use of AI in daily life and how it works. I like to share the top-ten list from Bernard Marr's article "The 10 Best Examples of How AI Is Already Used in Our Everyday Lives" (**bit.ly/3UbMZpN**), and then ask students to count how many of these they use regularly. This always makes for a great discussion—with students and other educators too!

7. Ask students to explain options for translating languages and communicating, specifying that they should provide non-technology and technology resources. Some examples could be a dictionary, a human translator, an app or web-based tool for translation, headphones, and other electronic translation devices that are available for real-time translation. What other ideas do they have?

8. Try a translation activity. Have students work in groups and choose a language. Provide students with text to translate, and depending on the length, allow 15–20 minutes for students to work in pairs/small groups as needed.

9. Have students share their responses after using an AI-powered translator.

10. Engage the class in a discussion of the translations. (Language teachers could use this to have students compare human versus computer-generated translation.) Based on the text provided, discuss words that may be confusing for a non-human translator, such as *bat, hang out, pen, invalid, resume*. How do humans know the difference and process the information? Can AI do the same thing? Why or why not?

11. Explore what might happen with the computer-assisted translation of the words listed above. How does context impact meaning and word choice? Who is better at understanding context?

12. If you have time, discuss the benefits of translators (time, communication is easier, reinforce language skills) and discuss accessibility (What are the benefits? Do these AI-powered translators save time and provide more support for students who are developing language skills?). Consider how many languages are spoken in the world and the impact of access to AI-powered translators in many tools being used in schools.

Choosing Tools and Activities

With so many resources available for teaching and learning about AI and more arriving each year, choosing which to share with your students can feel overwhelming. Remember, you don't have to be an expert to begin! Dive in and test things out before using them with your students or mentoring your colleagues. Remember, too, that you can all learn more together. Although I have favorites that I turn to frequently because of how much they offer for all grade levels and content areas, I also like to find and share new ones with my students. Some of my favorites are listed below. I've vetted these tools in my classroom so you can be more confident integrating them into yours.

✦ **AIClub:** AIClub is an online platform that not only offers K–12 curriculum but also a range of AI-related resources and activities for students. There are interactive lessons, coding challenges, and AI project ideas that you can explore for use in your classroom. Middle school students and younger learners can explore the AIClub Gym, which has some fun activities to develop an understanding of AI and how it works (**Figure 5.1**). A favorite of my class is Toonify, which changes your uploaded image or selfie into a cartoon character. Students can also explore projects that have been created by other students, which helps to spark curiosity and shows them that they too can create and innovate. AIClub also often hosts webinars and other professional resources for teachers to help you get started in your classroom.

FIGURE 5.1
Some of the activities available for students to explore in the AIClub Gym to learn about how AI works

Can an AI detect Hand poses?

Emotion Detection

Style Transfer

Telephone Game

✦ **AI World School:** This platform offers AI courses for learners ages 7–10, 11–13, and 14 and above (**Figure 5.2**). Older students can investigate courses on everything from virtual driverless cars to ethics, while fun activities give younger students a chance to understand how AI works as well as the benefits and concerns surrounding it. AIWS also launched its own self-driving car, the CV Pro, for students to learn about autonomous vehicles and become programmers. Beyond the courses themselves, this platform provides an opportunity to bring conversations about ethics into the classroom as students dive deep into the issues surrounding programming autonomous vehicles.

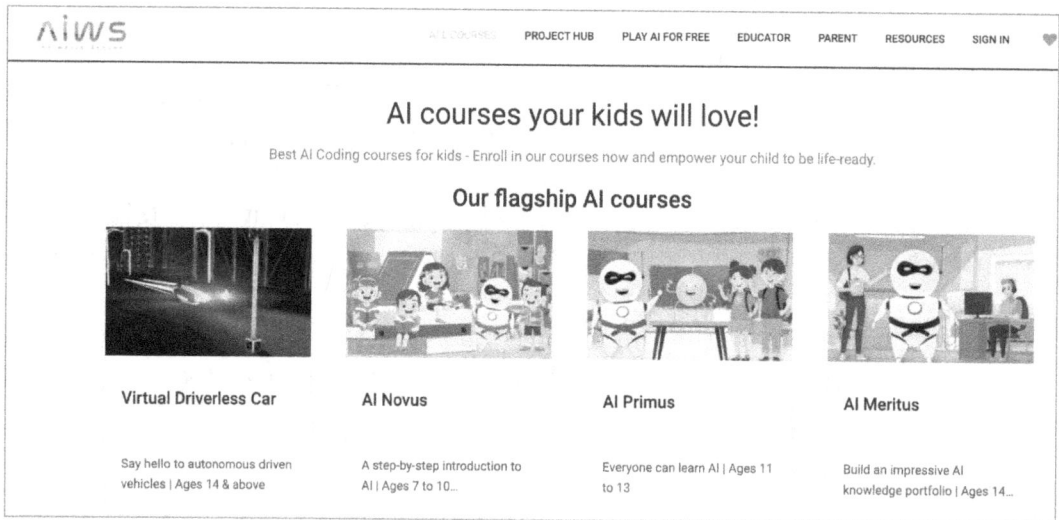

FIGURE 5.2
The courses available through AI World School (AIWS) that provide lessons for different grade level bands to learn about AI and complete activities and projects

✦ **Akinator:** This is a fun tool to explore in a class with older students and also a great way to demonstrate to other educators how algorithms sort through information and come up with a solution. Akinator is a "web genius" that asks questions in an effort to guess the famous real or fictional character, object, or animal that you choose. You respond to yes-no questions that it generates, and it uses your answers to sort through datasets based on prior game plays and then selects the best question to try next. It is fun to see the questions that it asks based on your responses and how many tries it takes to guess your choice. Try it, and see how long it takes and notice the changes in the questions that it asks you as it gets closer to guessing your character, animal, or object.

◆ **Code.org:** For years, Code.org has offered free interactive lessons, tutorials, and hands-on projects for K–12 students on many coding and STEM-related topics with the goal to spark interest in coding and STEM. Now it offers the *How AI Works* video series, which covers AI basics, machine learning, large language models, bias, and more. Students can find thousands of example projects and then create their own. Encourage students to brainstorm and design their own AI solution to a challenge they see in the world.

◆ **MIT AI Literacy Units for K–12:** The RAISE (Responsible AI for Social Empowerment and Education) initiative from MIT offers many great resources to help educators bring AI learning to the classroom. Available AI Literacy learning units include The A to Z of AI, AI & Ethics for Middle School, Careers in AI, Conversational AI Tools, Creativity & GANs or Dancing with AI for Middle School, Deep Fakes: The Ethics of Deep Fakes, How to Train Your Robot, and many more (**Figure 5.3**). Each unit comes with background information, activities, and even curriculum, and all materials are available under Creative Commons licensing. You can also find professional development resources for educators. This is a fantastic resource to explore when looking for reliable and up-to-date materials for classroom use.

FIGURE 5.3
Some of the options available through the MIT AI Literacy Units that help students learn about AI and develop essential AI literacy skills

- **The Ethics of Generative AI in the Classroom:** Created by Facing History & Ourselves, this mini-lesson for grades 6–12 focuses on the ethics surrounding the use of ChatGPT and DALL•E. The site provides an outline, activities, slides, and links to videos and other materials for teachers to promote discussion.

- **Google AI Experiments:** On this site from Google, there are a variety of AI experiments available that people have created using AI. Some of the areas of focus include arts, literacy, music, and more. I give students time to try some of the AI experiments, and after they spend time exploring, they can decide to design their own project. I often ask students to think about how AI could be used to enhance an aspect of life, whether in education, healthcare, or the business world, for a few examples. Students then draw what their AI model would be or write a description of how it would work. When students have a chance to create, they get more excited to learn about these technologies and consider the potential that AI has for transforming many areas of life and work.

- **Quick, Draw!:** In this online drawing game and artificial intelligence experiment, players sketch a prompted item on a digital canvas while the AI system attempts to recognize the drawing in real time (**Figure 5.4**). You're given six prompts and twenty seconds to draw each one. It is definitely an entertaining way to show how AI interprets human sketches, especially when demonstrating in front of students or other educators. I typically try to draw something in a completely unrelated shape to show how the neural network begins to eliminate objects as it analyzes the drawing. The project also contributes to AI research and data collection for improving machine-learning algorithms.

- **Human vs AI Test:** Can you identify which is human-created art, music, writing, or photos and which are AI-generated? On this site, you can find a variety of activities focused on AI. Some examples include "AI Test: Can you spot the difference?" and some AI-generated artwork, music, and photos to explore. At the bottom of the page, there is also an AI Test that takes about six minutes, in which you decide between AI- versus human-generated art, music, photos, and writing and also provide feedback as to why you made the choice. Once you finish the test, you can see how well you did for each of the four categories. You can click to check out the answers and access more activities around AI. You can extend the learning by reviewing some of the images or music, asking students to look closely and analyze what they see or hear. How do they determine if it was human or AI generated? It is definitely worth the time and a fun learning experience!

FIGURE 5.4
Quick, Draw! is a fun
way to teach students
about neural networks
and also engage in an
activity that helps
them to learn about AI.

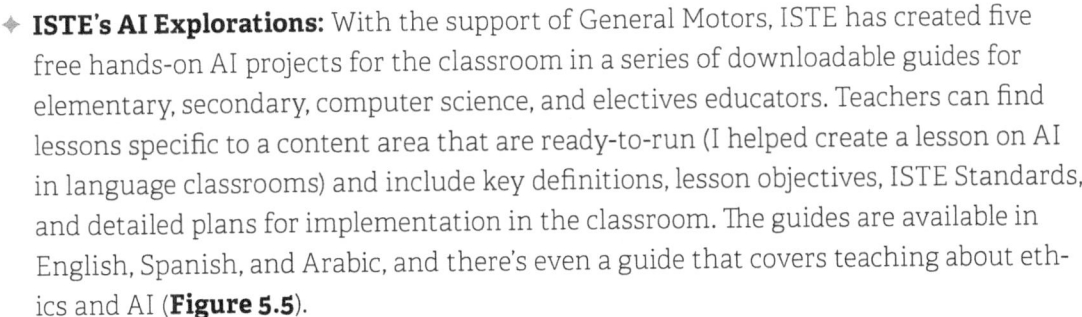

◆ **ISTE's AI Explorations:** With the support of General Motors, ISTE has created five free hands-on AI projects for the classroom in a series of downloadable guides for elementary, secondary, computer science, and electives educators. Teachers can find lessons specific to a content area that are ready-to-run (I helped create a lesson on AI in language classrooms) and include key definitions, lesson objectives, ISTE Standards, and detailed plans for implementation in the classroom. The guides are available in English, Spanish, and Arabic, and there's even a guide that covers teaching about ethics and AI (**Figure 5.5**).

FIGURE 5.5
The ISTE guides and
website provide lessons
and activities for var-
ious grade levels and
content areas, includ-
ing ethics.

◆ **Microsoft AI for Good:** This site offers many resources to help educators and students learn about and address global challenges and promote positive social impact. Specifically, it focuses on using AI technologies to tackle pressing issues such as environmental sustainability, accessibility, healthcare, and humanitarian efforts.

◆ **Microsoft Educator Center:** Here, Microsoft offers a wide range of free professional development courses, lesson plans, teaching materials, and tutorials available for educators to explore. Educators can also receive credentials for completing the modules and courses. In addition to courses for learning about AI technologies and how they are impacting education, you can find courses tailored to enhance digital literacy, classroom productivity, and student engagement.

◆ **Microsoft Designer:** Microsoft has a new AI image creator that uses DALL•E 3 and GPT-3.5 to generate digital artwork. You can use it for creating class materials, such as a hook for discussion, to get students involved in creating and evaluating generative AI capabilities, and for ideas to boost writing and speaking skills. Students do need an email to log in. Prompt templates to help get started are also available. If you're looking to explore, on X (formerly Twitter), many educators share templates that make it easier to generate a 3D avatar or image.

◆ ▶▶▶▶ First, I enjoyed filling in the blanks of the sample prompt templates that were created by other educators, a process that reminded me of Mad Libs. With Microsoft Designer, you can fill in details for a prompt template like *3D cartoon female with [color] hair, [color] eyes, and [mood].* You can also include additional items such as *riding a bike, holding an object,* or click Edit Entire Prompt to create your own prompt from scratch. It's a fun activity to try with students and generate some new avatars as well (**Figure 5.6**).

FIGURE 5.6
Microsoft Designer is a fun tool to get students and educators involved in creating with AI. Using the Mad Libs–style prompt templates makes it fun and quick to create a 3D cartoon character, for example.

A woman wearing a dark green V-neck sweater and a small dragonfly necklace, holding a black cat with green eyes in her right hand, with dark, long black hair with blue and purple highlights, rounded green eyes, looking happy

Share   Generate

◆ **Semantris:** Students can play this word-association game solo or collaboratively, challenging their vocabulary and critical thinking skills as they try to come up with words that are related to terms provided on their screen. As they play, they develop an understanding of how quickly AI sorts information and data to come up with an answer. For younger students, teachers can project the game on the board and ask students for ideas for words to type. It is a good way to push thinking and word association and help students develop an understanding of how AI works and brainstorm words to be able to succeed at the word game.

◆ **Wombo Dream:** Wombo Dream is an AI image generator that generates art based on the text you enter and style you choose. If you like the result, you can even purchase the image. In my class, we used it to generate images and talk about the quality of them, and then we tested different text prompts. Teachers could use this for a writing activity and ask students to create a fun description or talk about it with classmates.

A language educator may choose to have students describe it in the target language, for something different to explore and bring AI into the classroom.

In addition to these resources, there are also options available for learning about AI through robotics and coding. Some examples include KinderLab Robotics, which has the KIBO robot with AI lesson plans for early learners, and Marty the Robot from Robotical, which enables students to use Teachable Machine from Google within the Marty program.

For a listing of even more tools, as well as resources for learning, ready-made lessons, and even full curriculums, see Appendix B or scan the QR code at the end of the chapter.

EDUCATOR'S PERSPECTIVE: PUT RESOURCES TO WORK

By Kaywin Cottle, Computer Science Discoveries teacher, Burley Junior High, Idaho

For students learning about neural networks, I first introduce Quick, Draw!. We look at the examples that the neural network used to guess what students were drawing. We look for the patterns. We talk about diversity, such as possible age of the artist, skill level, and if the artist was possibly left- or right-handed. We look at the data sets and talk about possible bias. This opens up a lot more conversations about the field of AI in general and how limited the data sets are currently. We explore who probably has had a place at the table so far, what changes will have to be made for the future for AI to truly be representative, and what might happen if those changes do not occur. I then bring in the materials from the MIT AI Literacy curriculum for middle school to help the students further understand other ethical considerations. We next do the AI for Oceans unit in Code. org for the students to learn how to train AI, as well as some of the possibilities and outcomes for successful models and unsuccessful attempts. We then follow up with project-based learning activities in the ISTE AI Explorations curriculum.

⇗ Activity: Build a Chatbot

Understanding that AI is involved in a process and understanding how it works are two different things. As an educator, I believe it is important that we include opportunities for our students to experience creating and interacting with AI. Building a chatbot can be a fun activity for older students, and MIT App Inventor (**appinventor.mit.edu**) or Appy Pie (**appypie.com**) are great resources for getting started. There are many uses for chatbots, and students can come up with their own ideas for how a chatbot could be beneficial, whether they work individually or as a group. It is a good opportunity for them to build essential skills such as collaboration, critical thinking, creativity, and problem-solving.

Challenge them to think about how a chatbot could be used to benefit society whether in healthcare, business, or other settings. For older students, they can do some research into how chatbots are being used in these fields and share with classmates. Students can also work on teams to create a chatbot for younger students that helps them to practice a specific skill or has been programmed to answer questions related to a certain topic.

For example, students could build (or use) a chatbot to:

✦ Act as a study partner for students to help with homework and answer their questions.

✦ Help students practice their language skills by engaging them in conversation.

✦ Provide students with feedback on their writing assignments and suggest improvements.

✦ Help students improve their critical thinking skills by engaging them in thought-pro-voking discussions. Students could prompt the chatbot to portray a role or a character and engage in a debate, for example.

✦ Help students with mental health and wellness by providing them with coping strategies and resources. The MIT App Inventor offers a tutorial for how to do this (**appinventor.mit.edu/explore/resources/ai/therapist-bot**).

✦ Understand how ChatGPT works by creating their own ChatGPT app and engaging in conversations. The MIT App Inventor offers a tutorial for students in grades 6–12 (**appinventor.mit.edu/explore/resources/ai/chatGPT**).

Of course, be sure to check the safety guidelines for whatever platform you choose, and make sure student data is not compromised.

Key Takeaways

Remember that students must have opportunities to develop a greater understanding of emerging technologies, such as AI and its capabilities. (*ISTE Standard 1.1.d Empowered Learner*)

Students also need to connect their knowledge with real-world experiences and engage in problem-solving through the use of technology. (*ISTE Standard 1.3.d Knowledge Constructor*)

The ability to work through challenges and design solutions provides students with skills needed to adapt to changes that come from advancing technology. (*ISTE Standard 1.4.d Innovative Designer*)

As educators continue to adapt to changes in technology, staying current with research related to student learning and also sharing this knowledge with peers is essential. (*ISTE Standard 2.1.c Learner, 2.2.c Leader*)

Ongoing learning and sharing experiences with colleagues promote a positive learning culture for students and colleagues. (*ISTE Standard 2.3.b Citizen*)

Diving into new experiences and taking the risks with technology to learn with and from students will help educators stay current and relevant in their practice. (*ISTE Standard 2.4.b Collaborator*)

Looking for new experiences to dive into? Scan the QR code for a list of resources and tools.

tinyurl.com/ykt7c8z9

Questions for Reflection and Discussion

There are a lot of strategies and tools to explore that help educators to bring AI into their classrooms. Finding the right resources that provide support for students as they develop their skills can seem to be a huge task, but having a clear purpose in mind will make it easier. Don't hesitate to dive in and learn with and from students too! After reading this chapter, take a moment to reflect on what you've learned and consider:

✦ How might educators inspire students to identify real-world challenges that AI can address and to then think critically about potential solutions?

✦ How can AI projects provide opportunities for students to engage in interdisciplinary learning and problem-solving?

✦ What strategies can educators employ to balance guidance and independence as students become creators of AI-based projects?

✦ How can educators assess and recognize the unique skills and competencies that students develop through AI projects, beyond traditional assessments?

Share your ideas with me on X (formerly Twitter) @Rdene915 or post a message on LinkedIn.

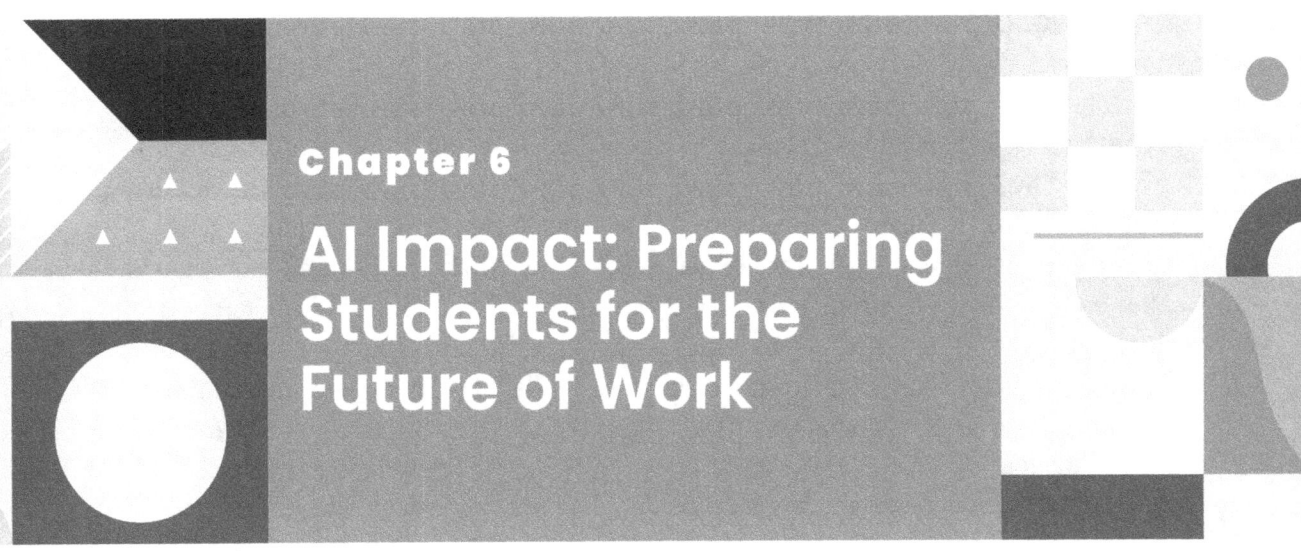

Chapter 6

AI Impact: Preparing Students for the Future of Work

The content of this chapter aligns with the following standards and indicators:

ISTE Student Standards

1.1.a, 1.1.d Empowered Learner

1. 3.d Knowledge Constructor

1.7.c Global Collaborator

ISTE Educator Standards

2.2.a Leader

2.3.a, 2.3.b Citizen

2.4.c Collaborator

AI TECHNOLOGY is steadily transforming how we live, learn, and work every single day. In 2013 Oxford University researchers estimated that 47% of all jobs in the United States were "at risk of automation over some unspecified number of years, perhaps a decade or two" (Kessler, 2023). In 2019 venture capitalist Kai-Fu Lee stated that 40% of the jobs will be replaced by AI by the year 2035 and referred to "repetitive jobs" as those that will be most likely to be automated (Axios, 2019). AI has already begun to revolutionize many industries such as business, finance, healthcare, and manufacturing. Many of the most common tasks are now automated, and customer questions are handled by chatbots, which causes concern over the potential loss of jobs for humans due to AI. However, AI will also bring about new opportunities, so we must adapt by developing and refining new skills. The World Economic Forum has predicted that 97 million jobs will be created by 2025 due to AI (Edison & Black, 2023). Many of those job roles will demand skills that are uniquely human. Similarly, the McKinsey Global Institute's 2023 report *Generative AI and the Future of Work in America* has predicted that by 2030, "up to 30 percent of hours currently worked across the US economy could be automated—a trend accelerated by generative AI" (Ellingrud et al., 2023). With predictions such as these, what will the demand be in 2030, and what do educators need to do to prepare students?

As educators, we play a pivotal role during this rapid growth: We must help students to understand what AI technology might mean for their future and the potential careers that they are considering. AI is reshaping the world of work, the in-demand jobs of the future, and the types of skills and competencies that students will need to thrive in it (Zinkula, 2024). In this chapter, we will explore what you can do to prepare students for the world of work's changing landscape. We will discuss the in-demand jobs of the future, the skills and competencies that students will need, and how you can leverage AI-related learning activities to help students develop these skills, such as critical thinking, creativity, and problem-solving. The activities, in particular, will be beneficial, enabling students to exercise the skills that many educators are worried will be hindered by the advancement in and the capabilities of AI.

AI's Impact on the Future Workplace

Educators have been talking about future-ready or future-focused skills for many years—but are we still focusing on those most in demand? We must continue to monitor what the in-demand skills are or are expected to be in order to provide students with opportunities to develop skills they may need due to the changes that will happen over the next five, ten, or fifteen years.

Many organizations conduct studies on the "in-demand" skills for jobs and the employment status in various sectors of work. Some also interview companies to find out how employment in their organization is changing and why. These studies can provide us with useful clues to guide us in our work as educators. Are different skill sets required? Are companies using AI to automate some of their processes? If so, what is the number of jobs that have been lost, and have new jobs been created? We can use these findings to adjust our teaching practices. Being informed will help us determine how to best prepare students and to get them involved in learning about the world of work, their available options in any field, and how AI might play a role in the work that they do in the future.

For example, the World Economic Forum (WEF) regularly publishes its *Future of Jobs Report* (which includes a "Job Skills Outlook" chapter) and many other valuable resources that examine the changing landscape of work, profile the industries affected, and make predictions for skills and jobs in demand for the future. The WEF has predicted that up to 25% of the jobs will change by the year 2027 (World Economic Forum, 2023). Some of the jobs that are on the rise are AI and machine learning specialists (which topped the list as the fastest growing job), computer programmers, data analysts, cybersecurity experts, and sustainability specialists. Researchers expect that generative AI will enhance rather than replace jobs and tasks in STEM-related fields, as well as professions such as business and legal. AI was listed as number three on the top ten list of business skill priorities for 2027 (World Economic Forum, 2023). A changing workplace requires a diverse set of skills and expertise.

WEF isn't the only predictor of change. In an IBM study regarding the effect of automation on jobs, 87% of the interviewed executives felt that generative AI would augment roles rather than replace them and that 40% of the workforce would have to reskill over the next three years as a result of AI changes (Ortiz, 2023). According to the Pew Research Center's Social & Demographic Trends Project, "Because AI could be used either to replace or complement what workers do, it is not known exactly which or how many jobs are in peril" (Kochhar, 2023). The PEW study looked at forty-one essential work-related activities in 873 occupations taken from the U.S. Department of Labor's Occupational Information Network. So how do we prepare students to be competitive and adaptable to changing conditions in work?

According to the Pew Research Center, it is important to determine the likelihood that a task or job could be either replaced or complemented by AI and whether it is a low, medium, or high likelihood (Kochhar, 2023). Automation has replaced jobs and will continue to do so, perhaps even at a faster pace due to the rise of generative AI tools available for use in all areas of work. According to the McKinsey Global Institute (2023), "With Generative AI added to the picture, 30% of hours worked today could be automated by 2030" (Ellingrud et al., 2023). Although this sounds like a hugely negative impact, their report shares that rather than completely eliminating jobs, generative AI may be used to enhance the way that certain professionals in business, creative, legal, and STEM-related fields do their work. Education and workforce training are also predicted to see an increase in automation due to generative AI. Not all jobs will be lost, as some will be enhanced with this technology, and entirely new jobs will appear. One estimate predicts 12 million jobs will be created rather than replaced as a result of AI and 97 million specialists will be needed in AI-related fields by 2025 (Simon, 2022).

So where can students apply their skills, and what steps must we take as educators to help them to prepare? We need to create opportunities for them to become the creators of AI, to learn how to code, to design new technologies that will make an impact on not only their learning experience but for the future. Students also need to understand the impact of these technologies on society. In other words, schools must provide opportunities for all students to learn about and understand how AI works. To help, Dave Touretzky, the founder of **AI4K12.org**, created a robust site full of resources for educators. In addition to an email forum for sharing ideas and asking questions, AI4K12 provides links to AI learning tools, blogs, books, lessons, videos, and more. It is continually updated with new materials for educators, which is essential, especially with this rapidly advancing technology. Touretzky has stated "It's important that children be given accurate information about AI so they can understand the technology that is reshaping our lives" (Wdadmin, 2018).

As we see changes happening, we need to continue to learn about the types of jobs and skill sets that are in demand, most likely as a result of AI and automation. In a 2021 *Forbes* article, Anurag Gurtu shared insights on five industries that were (and still are) seeing increased benefits from artificial intelligence: automotive, ecommerce, finance, healthcare, and transportation and travel. Let's take a closer look at each, as well as some related activities to try with your students. (For additional examples of industry connections, scan the QR code at the end of the chapter.)

Automotive Industry

According to Abdelmohsen (2023), 33 million self-driving cars will be on the road by 2040. Artificial intelligence enables such cars to navigate roads, avoid collisions, and analyze the flow of traffic. Skilled professionals are needed to evaluate the effectiveness of this technology for reducing the number of accidents and evaluate its impact on safety for drivers. Our students can develop the necessary skills for this role by learning how the algorithms work and how these decisions are made. They also need to realize that they may be the ones who are creating and working with this technology in the future.

The Virtual Driverless Car course from AI World School, which I use with my STEAM class, is a great resource to learn more about how self-driving cars are programmed and the relevant issues, such as ethics, involved (**Figure 6.1**). You could also check AutoAuto Lab's Python & AI with Autonomous Cars, which offers virtual and physical cars (**Figure 6.2**), and the PASCO Coding with Vehicle Sensor Technologies Kit. With tools like these, students can learn about AI, practice coding with Python, and engage in important conversations about how these vehicles might impact the world. The hands-on experiences also give students a chance to dive into creating more with AI and focus on ethical considerations.

FIGURE 6.1
The curriculum covered in the Virtual Driverless Car course from AI World School

FIGURE 6.2
The lessons in the AutoAuto course for students to work through and learn about virtual autonomous cars

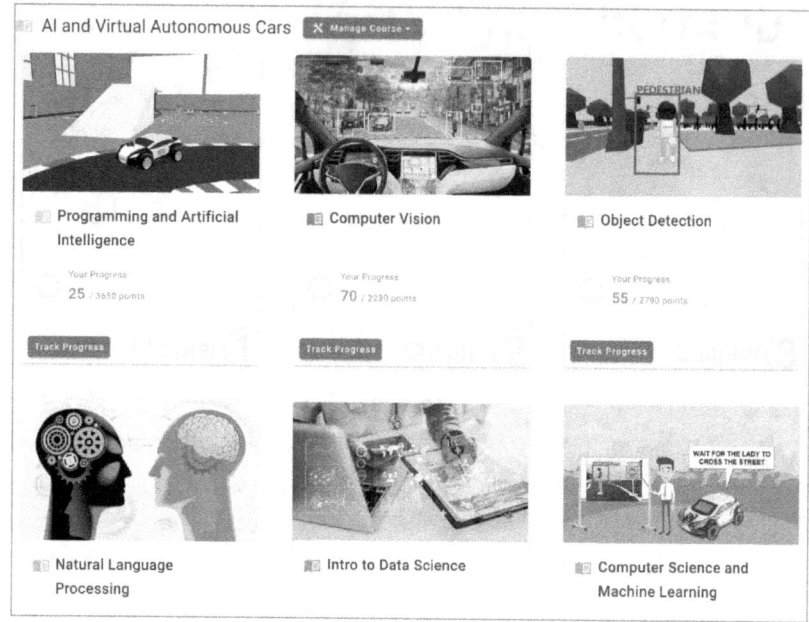

FIGURE 6.2
The lessons in the AutoAuto course for students to work through and learn about virtual autonomous cars

◥ Activity: Self-Driving Cars and Ethics

Discuss self-driving cars with students, and you may be surprised at their responses to the idea of having such a vehicle. I expected many of my students would want one, but very few said that they would be interested in having this type of technology available to them. The biggest reasons? They would not feel safe in the vehicle and would not want to trust the driving and their safety to AI. You can then dive into questions such as what are some of the most important considerations that programmers need to make? How do they create the program so that the car would know what to do when confronted with a dangerous situation? This is a great way to bring ethics into the class conversation. Another resource, **MoralMachine.net**, presents students with thirteen pairs of scenarios involving self-driving cars (**Figure 6.3**). Through these scenarios, students must consider an appropriate action to take based on different factors. The options include deciding to swerve to avoid pedestrians of various types at the risk to passengers in the car or to protect the passengers at the expense of pedestrians. After the scenarios are completed, students see a breakdown of the impact of their choices and have an option to share some of the factors (age, gender, obeyance of traffic signals, etc.) that affected their decisions with the study's creators. Students can also submit a scenario to be used as well. As the site's name suggests, many ethical discussions could spring from this activity, and it involves students in a discussion about ethics which is more authentic for them, especially if they design the scenarios.

FIGURE 6.3
Moral Machine enables students to create their own decision scenarios for self-driving cars and to consider the ethical issues involved.

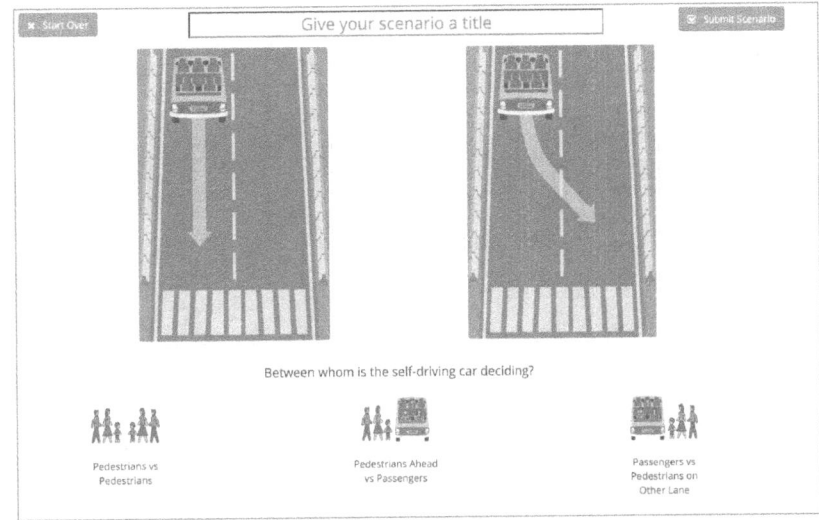

Ecommerce

The impact of AI on ecommerce isn't hard to see. Have you searched something on Google or a shopping site to then find ads for similar products popping up on the other websites that you interact with? AI algorithms make this possible by analyzing your browsing history, past purchases, and preferences, then recommending related products for you. Also, chatbots embedded in websites enable customers to ask questions or open a ticket for assistance with an order and receive a response in far less time compared to waiting online to speak to a person. Some of these chatbots are also programmed to then connect the customer to a human customer service agent to provide further assistance. If you have not yet interacted with a chatbot on a website, test out its functionalities by asking questions and then type *agent* to see how it decides to transfer you to a human agent. Consider the benefits and any potential negatives of these capabilities.

◥ Activity: Customer Service Chatbots Debate

Take time to discuss the benefits or engage in pros and cons with students. An activity such as this is very beneficial for students to consider some guiding questions: Is it helpful for chatbots to be available to interact with the customer? What are the negatives that come with having this technology available, and how does it impact humans? You could consider dividing the class into two groups of "for" and "against" this type of technology. Together they then have to come up with key points to present their position to the other group. Also remind students that they need to find some resources to back up their position statement.

Finance

AI can process large amounts of data and instantly complete tasks and transactions that in the past took hours or days and multiple people to complete—a perfect fit in the world of finance. For example, investment firms use "robo advisors" to build personalized portfolios and profiles for investors without any human interaction (Johnson, 2023), while banks use AI-powered technology to monitor accounts for errors and potential fraud. Fraud detection algorithms monitor credit card transactions for purchases made outside of the card holder's typical geographical area or purchasing habits. If one appears, the card holder receives an automated call, text, or email as a warning. Using an online banking app, the consumer can then approve or deny the charge, and even freeze their card to prevent additional transactions—all without human intervention.

Activity: Research and Consider

Start by asking students about how they think AI is being used in the financial sector. Prompt them with different jobs or tasks that involve finances, and ask how AI does or could potentially save time and benefit those working in the financial sector. Students can then do some research with a partner or in small groups to find real-world examples of the use of AI in finance. Ask students to identify some common transactions and consider how algorithms and the power of AI facilitate the transactions in far less time.

Healthcare

Artificial intelligence has the potential to bring about significant changes in the healthcare industry. Leveraging machine learning and the ability to quickly analyze massive amounts of data, AI can review medical and diagnostic testing faster with greater accuracy and efficiency than traditional methods, which can lead to earlier (and potentially life-saving) diagnoses and treatment of medical conditions. Using machine-learning algorithms to analyze x-rays and tissue samples for pathology can help doctors identify problems more quickly and provide critical care for patients. AI that has been trained on data to know what a normal lung x-ray looks like, for example, can rapidly spot anomalies that indicate a patient may have pneumonia, COVID-19, cancer, or another condition. Of course, we all benefit from the human touch of a doctor or other medical professional to review the findings and discuss them with the patient, but AI-powered medical devices can give doctors new insights into patient needs for faster or more targeted care. Students considering careers in healthcare very well may be relying on AI for some components of the work that they do. Understanding how it works and how to evaluate its results will be key.

In the mental healthcare field, chatbots offer a way to make services more accessible. Founded by psychologist Alison Darcy, Woebot Health (**woebothealth.com**) offers chatbots, including one for teens 13–17, designed to help users work through some mental challenges. "Rather than sharing intimate details with another person," Darcy explained, "young people, who have spent their whole lives interacting with technology, could feel more comfortable working through their problems with a machine" (Keierleber, 2022). Some teens reported positive effects and preferred the chatbot to speaking with a counselor, stating "It's a robot. It's objective. It can't judge me" (Keierleber, 2022). It can, however, give teens experience with natural language processing (NLP), which is valuable in additional ways. Some advanced chatbots can even use sentiment analysis (analyzing digital text to determine the emotional tone of the message) to interpret language and mood to offer a more personalized response and interaction with the person. Natural language processing is also being used to work with people diagnosed with bipolar disorder (Kennedy, 2022), and research indicates that "language analysis can be used to assist in and improve the provision of care for people" with the condition (Harvey et al., 2022).

✖ Activity: Healthcare Careers and AI

Ask students to choose a career in the healthcare or mental health field and explore how AI is involved and what the impact is. You can also prompt them to come up with ways that AI could be used and what the potential benefits and concerns could be. An activity like this could be done with individual students as part of a problem-based learning experience or could be done in small groups, which will also help to boost engagement in learning and the building of essential skills.

⚑ Activity: Chatbots for Mental Wellness

In a class discussion, ask your students what they think about the use of chatbots for mental health and wellness. Focus on the ethics behind the use of these technologies and also the importance of privacy. What are the concerns and benefits of these technologies? Ask students to think of additional ideas to share. Through these discussions, we can also help students develop empathy and increase awareness of some issues being faced by people in the world.

Transportation and Travel

How many times have you traveled and used Google to look for restaurants, stores, theaters, or other attractions "near me?" More than 80% of people regularly use their phones to search restaurants and landmarks to visit (Restaurant Engine, 2024), and AI algorithms provide the answers. While you follow its turn-by-turn directions, Google Maps algorithms scan the roads and environs, adapting and providing information about upcoming traffic delays and nearby businesses in real time. Similarly, the Uber and Lyft ride-sharing apps provide estimates of your travel time and the cost because the AI functionality enables them to do an analysis of the traffic patterns in real time. For example, Uber uses a deep learning algorithm called DeepETA to predict demand and travel times (Hu, et al., 2022).

⚑ Activity: Travel Reflections

Ask students about their travel experience. With their families, do they rely on services such as Uber or Lyft for travel? In looking for restaurants, local attractions, or information on historical facts, are they using Google or AI-powered apps or even simply voice-to-text to save time? Are there AI-powered tools that promote accessibility for travelers who may not speak a language or may require assistance with vision? Some examples to look at include Google Translate and Seeing AI. Another activity to try is The Uber Game (**ig.ft.com/uber-game**), which is a bit more interactive. The Uber Game helps students develop an understanding of finances and also the work of an Uber driver (**Figure 6.4**).

FIGURE 6.4
In The Uber Game, students work through questions and decisions in an effort to meet financial responsibilities and become a successful Uber driver.

What This Means for Students

During the rapid switch to remote learning during the pandemic in 2020, use of, interest in, and spending on artificial intelligence increased. It's still going up, fueled by a greater focus on reducing the burden of administrative tasks on educators, the need for personalized learning, and a rise in the demand for "intelligent solutions to improve students' academic performance in the region" (Nagel, 2023). There are many questions about how artificial intelligence will impact education in the future. P&S Intelligence predicted that global spending on AI in education would grow from the $2.13 billion spent in 2022 to $25.77 billion in 2030 (Nagel, 2023). Although these estimates are for worldwide spending, North America is the largest user of AI in education (Nagel, 2023). Beyond the education field, AI spending is rising as well. In 2022 the U.S. government spent $3.3 billion on AI contracts, according to a Stanford University study (Krishan, 2023). AI spending in education is estimated to reach $23.82 billion by 2030 (GlobeNewswire, 2023)—an increase due to the increased interest in AI-powered intelligent resources and platforms for students. Similarly, studies conducted by the International Data Corporation (IDC) predicted that worldwide AI spending would jump to $154 billion in 2023 (Feger, 2023).

As educators, these statistics matter because we have to create experiences for our students that help them to understand AI technologies. Regardless of what our students decide to do in the future, it will involve this technology. Some students may become the creators of the solutions and smart machines that we will need in the future, while others may find their jobs augmented (or replaced) by currently emerging technologies.

Students will need a variety of skill sets to be prepared. According to the World Economic Forum, "an eye for detail, creative problem-solving skills, a collaborative mindset, and an ability to deal with ambiguity and complexity" will be essential as 1 billion jobs will be transformed by technology in the next ten years (S & George, 2020). The organization's report *Jobs of Tomorrow: Mapping Opportunity in the New Economy* forecast an influx of jobs in such technical areas as artificial intelligence, data analytics, and cloud computing, however, it also stated that "demand for both 'digital' and 'human' factors is driving growth in the professions of the future" (World Economic Forum, 2020).

As part of your professional learning, in conversations with other educators, and when designing lessons, consider:

✦ What do we need to know about the future of AI and how can we prepare ourselves so that we can prepare our students?

✦ How can we create the right learning opportunities to build student skills for jobs that may not exist yet?

✦ What types of opportunities do we need to provide for them?

✦ What are some ideas as to how AI will be used in different types of work?

▶▶▶▶ Some steps to take towards the answers are simple. Discuss what artificial intelligence is and where students see it used in daily life, then shift the conversation to explore careers and student interests to determine where AI is already having an impact. Conducting a career study and learning about how or if AI can replace some of the human component of those jobs will help students to better prepare for jobs of the future. Of course, consider what potential concerns exist surrounding AI as well.

We need to create a space for students to explore, develop their own understanding, interact with, and then create their own AI. Giving students the chance to learn in a more hands-on or self-directed manner will make a difference. To develop essential problem-solving and collaborative skills, students need the chance to try something, fail at it, adapt, set new goals, and repeat. With the many resources available (see Appendix B or scan the QR code at the end of the chapter), learners at all grade levels can design apps, create new innovations with AI, and develop critical skills for their futures. For example, knowing how to code is a skill that is marketable to many high-demand careers.

The Skills Students Will Need

To prepare students for the future workplace, we must equip them with skills and competencies that go beyond traditional knowledge acquisition. Some of the skills that will be essential in the future, regardless of the impact of AI, are:

+ **Adaptability:** Being able to adapt to a world of work that may change rapidly is key. Students may need to make job shifts or learn new skills—and in very little time. Think of how quickly everyone in education (and beyond) had to adapt during the pandemic! Being able to adjust to changing and sometimes challenging situations is key.

+ **Collaboration:** Working with others has been on the top ten skills list from the World Economic Forum for years. Teamwork is a key part of many jobs, whether coworkers are in the same workspace or spread across the country. Being able to communicate and collaborate, as well as understanding how to best leverage technologies to do so is vital.

+ **Critical thinking:** In learning activities, we must encourage students to analyze, evaluate, and question the information they are receiving. With access to so many online and AI-generated resources, students need to develop critical thinking skills to be successful. Being able to discern information and knowing how to process and apply it will continue to be a skill that is in demand. Just as early spell checkers could tell you the word *giraffe* was spelled correctly but only a human proofreader could determine whether the word made sense in the document's context, so too will humans still be needed to evaluate the effectiveness of AI tools in the future.

+ **Creativity:** In a world of emerging technologies, students need opportunities to think outside the box and innovate. Use methods such as project- or problem-based learning to have students design creative and innovative solutions to challenges in the world. The use of generative AI can help to spark creativity, but it should not replace opportunities for students to be creative nor for teachers to dive into being creative as well in providing materials and opportunities for students. Generative AI could produce a written or visual story prompt for students to exercise their imagination with, for example, but students should not rely on it to write the story itself. Let it be the spark for student creativity!

+ **Problem-solving:** For students to be able to adapt, they must be flexible and develop problem-solving skills that will help them to navigate difficult situations. Provide them with complex situations, and guide them to find solutions. Adding or changing variables in a challenge gives students the opportunity to adapt and collaborate on a new solution, all while putting their creativity and critical-thinking skills to work.

Real-World AI Learning Opportunities

According to businessman and *Shark Tank* investor Mark Cuban, "AI will dominate the workplace, and to be successful, people are going to have to understand it" (Sauer, 2022). In collaborations between industry and education, many students are learning to understand AI in amazing and innovative ways. Backing up its founders' words, the Mark Cuban Foundation partners with businesses across the U.S. to host free Intro to Artificial Intelligence Bootcamps that enable high school students to learn about AI, machine learning, large language models, and ethical issues, as well as build their own app and meet adults currently working in STEM fields.

Meanwhile, Create Labs offers opportunities for students to work with its AI ambassador C.L.Ai.R.A. (Create Labs Artificial Intelligence Rendered Assistant) and her creators at their own schools. C.L.Ai.R.A. was modeled as an Afro-Latina woman, and her voice was based on that of Amber Ivey, a well-known member of Black Women in Technology (Create Labs, 2023). The purpose of C.L.Ai.R.A., which has been called "most powerful AI out there," is to "help communities with their needs while representing people of color" (Wilson, 2022).

▶▶▶▶ YouTube features many videos of C.L.Ai.R.A. speaking that you can share with your students, or share an image of her from magazine cover or news interview. Can students tell that she is a humanoid? Does she look, move, and sound like a person? If so, how? What are the ways that students can identify a humanoid from a human? What do students think about a humanoid giving a talk or presenting at an event? Take time to discuss the benefits of having an assistant like this, as well as what negatives might come with it.

Help Students Discover Career and Skill Interests

▶▶▶▶ For our students, understanding the career areas where we will see growth or decreases as a result of AI is important, and developing skills in multiple areas will be key to success in a job market that will continue to change. To help them prepare, make time in class to discuss with students what jobs they think might be impacted, and how AI might cause a change in tasks done in a certain occupation or potentially the elimination of a type of job. Share with them some of the statistics we discussed earlier, look at the job predictions and the skills available from the World Economic Forum, and investigate the *Learn to Code with Me* blog's list of eighteen most in demand tech skills (**learntocode-with.me/posts/tech-skills-in-demand**). Give them some choices to explore to see if they have an interest in pursuing careers in these fields. Students can share what they find and together learn about the great demand for people to fill these jobs.

⚡Activity: Will Robots Take My Job?

To think about the future of work, visit the Will Robots Take my Job? website (**willro-botstakemyjob.com**) with your students, or ask students to come up with a list of jobs and then gather the information to share with them in class. My classes find it fun to test jobs—those they think could be replaced by AI and automation and those they don't think could be replaced. The site returns an automation risk percentage for each job, as well as information on growth, wages, and more for the job. This data can lead to a class conversation as to why students believe a job can or cannot be replaced, as well as give students a chance to learn about their career possibilities as they prepare for their future. The activity also can provide insight into what our students' interests are so that we can use that to design more authentic learning opportunities for them. It may lead to us trying different methods in our classroom, such as genius hour or project-based learning, or career exploration to connect our content with emerging technologies like AI. For elementary educators who are interested in AI activities but wonder about how to bring them in, this is a great way to connect AI into class discussions related to multiple types of content. A caution is to always make sure this website and any related content or pop-up ads are age-appropriate. An extension is to seek professionals to speak about these careers as well and if AI has impacted them.

AI and Careers Lesson Plans

Here are lesson plans for three more activities you can use to help students understand AI's impact on the workplace and the future.

❦ Activity: AI Research

Objective: To help students understand how to find information related to the impact of AI and its use in the workplace.

Divide students into groups and have them locate at least one news article, one website, and one video about AI and its uses in the workplace. Students should then summarize the key points and discuss the potential benefits and challenges of AI in the workplace.

Once the groups have finished, engage the class in a discussion where each group presents their findings. You can even have a debate, which is great for helping students develop speaking skills and learn about advocacy, as well as how to listen to one another and build awareness of others' perspectives. If you have concerns about creativity, critical thinking, and problem-solving, this type of activity can address those skills!

Extension: Depending on the age of students, they could then use a generative AI tool to create an infographic, image, or other media to represent their findings and share with the school community.

❦ Activity: AI and Career Exploration

Objective: To help students discover potential career options related to AI and learn about the skills that are required.

Depending on the age of students, you can provide a list of AI-related jobs (cybersecurity experts, data scientists, computer programmers, machine learning engineers, etc.) or have students find their own by doing some research. Another good idea is to assign a specific job to each group and have them research the job description, responsibilities, and required qualifications for the job, and then find information on the demand for these jobs.

Once the groups have finished, engage the class in a discussion during which each group presents their findings. Encourage students to ask questions and make suggestions as to the benefits of these jobs or predict how the job market may change as a result. To close out the activity, ask students if they are surprised by any of the information that they learned during this activity. Depending on the course you teach, you could focus on a type of career that aligns with the content area taught. Another idea is to potentially have students track the growth or decline in their chosen career throughout the school year or to stay aware of any news regarding changes to it as a result of AI.

❧ Activity: AI and Automation Simulation

Objective: To help students understand automation and its current and potential future impact on various occupations.

Have students create their own fictitious company, and assign each member of the group to have a role in the company. Some possibilities include customer service agent, data entry, managers, and other relevant roles.

Students should then create their own AI-powered enhancement for their role or bring in an automated system that exists, and then consider how it impacts their specific role.

Once the groups have finished, engage the class in a discussion about the impact of automation and how they would adapt. Can they predict any potential loss of jobs or changes that might occur in the future with some companies as a result of automation? Also have them consider the benefits of automation. To bring it back to future-preparedness, students can also consider the types of skills that will be needed regardless of the likelihood of automation.

❧ Activity: AI-Powered Sustainable Solutions

Objective: To teach students about the United Nations Sustainable Development Goals (SDGs) and find ways to address the goals by using AI-powered technology.

To get started, introduce students to the Sustainable Development Goals (**sdgs.un.org/goals**) and have a brief discussion about each of the seventeen goals (**Figure 6.5**). After the discussion, either break students into groups or ask students to select one or two goals that they are interested in.

FIGURE 6.5
The seventeen global Sustainable Development Goals set by the United Nations

Once students are in groups, they should work together to brainstorm and design a solution using AI that will help to address the SDG challenge. For example, if students select SDG 2 Zero Hunger, could AI be used to identify patterns and trends to help farmers make informed decisions about planting and irrigation? Challenge each team to design a solution whether they create something using generative AI or simply draw their proposed solution.

Each group should then present their project to the class and be prepared to answer questions from their peers.

Some potential questions for all groups:

✦ How did AI enhance the potential impact of the solutions your team created?

✦ What challenges did you encounter while brainstorming or designing AI-powered solutions?

✦ What are the potential risks and benefits of AI in addressing sustainability challenges? Are there any ethical considerations?

Key Takeaways

Prominent research and studies agree: AI will continue to impact many areas of the world of work. Our task as educators is to help to prepare students. Because of the predicted increase in the use of AI, our students need to have a variety of learning experiences that will spark curiosity and provide insight into future career interests.

As educators, we need to continue to explore emerging technologies and provide opportunities that not only help students develop the skills needed to adjust as technology changes but also to collaborate and co-learn with students. (*ISTE Standards 2.2.a and 2.2.c Leader, 2.4.b and 2.4.c Collaborator*)

We should also mentor students in the ethical and responsible use of AI tools and create opportunities for students in all classrooms to explore the impact of AI in their world. (*ISTE Standards 2.2.c. Leader, 2.3.a and 2.3.b Citizen*)

We can help our students develop a greater understanding of AI and emerging technologies through opportunities to explore its impact on various sectors of work and life. (*ISTE Standards 1.1.d Empowered Learner, 1.3.d Knowledge Constructor, 1.7.c Global Collaborator*)

Designing activities for students to work independently or collaboratively as they seek information and use this new knowledge to understand real-world issues is essential. For a list of tools, organizations, and ready-made lessons to help you, scan the QR code.

tinyurl.com/ykt7c8z9

Questions for Reflection and Discussion

We have covered a variety of areas in the world of work where AI is making an impact. As educators, we need to continue to learn about the skills in demand and consider how to prepare students with the right opportunities that will enable them to adapt and be flexible as changes in jobs and the skills required evolve. After reading this chapter, take a moment to reflect on what you've learned and consider:

✦ How can schools adapt their curriculum to foster the skills and competencies required for success in an AI-driven job market?

- How might schools and educators collaborate with industries and businesses to provide students with real-world exposure to AI applications and job opportunities?

- What role can student agency play in shaping AI-related learning pathways and future career choices?

- How can educators empower students to become active contributors and problem-solvers in the evolving landscape of AI-driven work opportunities?

Share your ideas with me on X (formerly Twitter) @Rdene915 or post a message on LinkedIn.

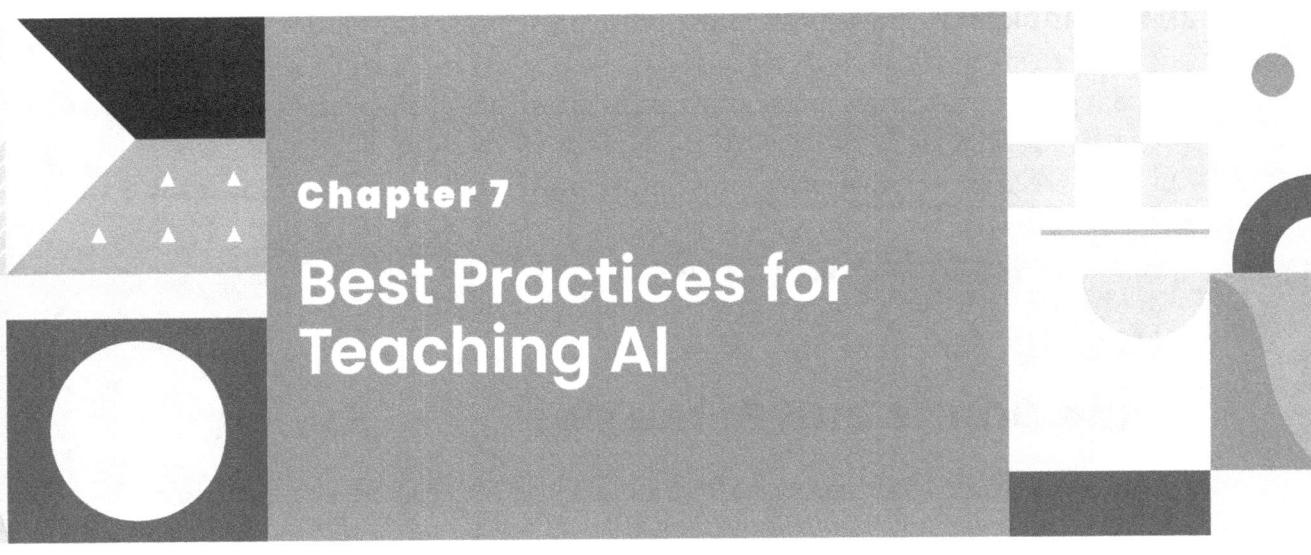

Chapter 7

Best Practices for Teaching AI

The content of this chapter aligns with the following standards and indicators:

ISTE Student Standards

1.1.d Empowered Learner

1.2.b, 1.2.d Digital Citizen

1.3.b Knowledge Constructor

1.5.d Computational Thinker

ISTE Educator Standards

2.1.c Learner

2.2.b Leader

2.3.d Citizen

2.4.a Collaborator

IN THIS BOOK, we have discussed what artificial intelligence is, defined its key terms, and explored many examples of how it is used in every life. In our schools, we need to provide opportunities for our students to understand this technology, its power, and its potential impact on the future of work. As educators, we must continue to learn and do our best to keep up with changes we may see in our work and explore new tools that we can bring into our classrooms to not only enhance the work we do, but to provide more supports and opportunities for our students. As you and your students embark on your own AI journey, here are a few reminders to help it go smoothly.

Some Don'ts and Some Dos

Let's recap some of the key takeaways from our discussions. Keep these considerations in mind when teaching about artificial intelligence in the classroom and choosing tools for and planning activities with students. First, the don'ts:

✦ **Don't feel like you have to be an expert to start.** Yes, you need to understand the basics of AI and have a few resources to begin exploring. From there, embrace the learning opportunities with your students!

✦ **Don't use AI to replace teachers.** AI should not replace the important human inter-actions between students and teachers, or between students. Social and emotional learning requires authentic human connections. We need to continue to build interper-sonal skills and collaborate. Using AI to replace teachers can have negative consequences on students' learning and development. While AI can provide personalized learning experiences and support, it cannot replace the human interaction and emotional con-nection that teachers provide. Students need guidance and mentorship from teachers to develop critical thinking skills, social and emotional skills, and a sense of community in the classroom. AI lacks the ability to connect with students on a personal level and adapt to their individual needs, which is crucial for effective education.

✦ **Don't believe that AI is always right.** After all, it was programmed by humans, and the algorithms they created are susceptible to error. Also, because we may not know where a tool's training information was pulled from, the sources may be unreliable, outdated, or biased. The importance of close reading, fact checking, and verifying the accuracy of data received is crucial. Guide students to understand how to access infor-mation, but then to analyze, evaluate, and interpret that information for reliability before using it.

- ✦ **Don't overlook bias in AI algorithms.** It is important to look at the output from the prompts used with a tool like ChatGPT and other AI-powered tools. Take time to regularly review and address potential biases to ensure fair treatment of all students.

- ✦ **Don't forget about privacy and security.** Do not allow unnecessary student data to be collected or share sensitive information with third-party AI providers without having data protection measures in place. Read the fine print and make sure that each platform or resource addresses how any data collected will be used or shared. Keep personally identifiable information out of any prompts entered into AI-powered tools.

- ✦ **Don't plagiarize with AI.** Do not simply copy and paste AI-generated content into your work without proper attribution, citation, or original input. We know students and even educators may incorporate the output in their work and use it as their own writing. Not only will the information likely contain inaccuracies, but also we must model giving proper credit to a source. Using AI as a tool for information is okay, but we need to infuse our knowledge to expand on the results, while being mindful of citing the resources properly. When using ChatGPT, you and students can cite its results in APA, Chicago Manual of Style, or MLA formats.

- ✦ **Don't develop an overreliance on AI.** Avoid replacing human teachers or human tasks with AI entirely. The human interactions in education and in work are essential for continued growth and building relationships. Decide how to best leverage the technology to enhance or facilitate the work that is done by humans or that requires innately human characteristics.

- ✦ **Don't use AI for excessive standardization.** Avoid using AI to excessively standardize education, as it might hinder creativity and diverse learning approaches. There are many tools available that make it easier to create an assessment and analyze the data with little human intervention. As educators, however, we should strive to personalize learning to better reach our students. To do so, it is essential that we understand where our students are in the learning journey so we are able to provide the support they need to best meet their specific learning needs, pace, and interests.

- ✦ **Don't forget about transparency.** Do not implement AI systems without explaining the *why* behind the use of these tools to students and educators. Transparency is important when bringing technology or new methods into our schools. Transparency builds trust and understanding, which are essential to forming a supportive and thriving learning community.

+ **Don't use only AI for grading.** Avoid relying solely on AI for grading assessments, as it may overlook qualitative aspects of student learning and development.

+ **Don't create a digital divide.** When implementing AI tools, focus on access. Don't use AI tools without ensuring equal access to technology for all students.

+ **Don't ignore student input.** It is important to involve students in the decision-making process. Ask them what their thoughts are about the use of any AI-powered tools. Their insights are valuable for shaping AI integration and we learn a lot from them too.

Now, consider some important reminders on what you *should* do:

+ **Do use AI programs as smart search engines** that present information in ways that are easy to read and understand. (But always fact check!)

+ **Do ask AI programs for clarification** or explanations when you need help.

+ **Do generate ideas**, topics, and writing prompts using AI programs.

+ **Do be transparent.** Attribute AI text and images properly when you use them in your work. It is important to model this for our students.

+ **Do collaborate with AI.** Use AI programs as collaborative tools to brainstorm ideas, enhance creativity, and assist in the research process.

+ **Do learn from AI.** Leverage AI programs for supplementary learning, accessing tutorials, and gaining deeper insights into complex subjects or topics such as AI itself and its underlying concepts. It can be a virtual tutor or assistant.

+ **Do leverage AI for accessibility.** Use AI tools to make educational content more accessible, such as providing text-to-speech or translation services, or designing differentiated resources for diverse learners.

+ **Do model ethical AI use.** Encourage discussions about the ethical use of AI in the classroom and how it can benefit education.

+ **Do use AI for feedback** on assignments and assessments to identify areas of improvement and guide your learning.

+ **Do have fun exploring** the tools available and gaining a better understanding of how AI can be beneficial in education and the world. Have fun learning with students!

Questions for Reflection and Discussion

As we reach the end of this final chapter, take a moment to reflect on what you've learned throughout the book. Would you answer those first questions from Chapter 1 the same way now?

+ What concerns do you have when it comes to AI?

+ What are some areas where you believe that AI will help you in your classroom or school?

+ As an educator, why do you think it is important to learn about AI?

+ How do you plan to start teaching about or using AI in your classroom?

After reflecting on these questions, think about how you will apply what you have learned and how it will impact your classroom now and in the future. Consider:

+ What will you change about your practice due to the capabilities of AI?

+ Think about five years from now. What will education look like, and how will AI play a role?

+ How will you share what you have learned with colleagues and students?

+ What advice can you offer other educators who are just starting their AI journey?

Looking Ahead

Embrace the benefits of AI-powered tools while exercising a healthy skepticism. Continue to be mindful of the ethical concerns surrounding them, and always review the privacy and safety guidelines provided by companies or organizations to make sure they are in compliance with applicable regulations. Continue to evaluate the information that you receive when using generative AI tools and encourage your students to do the same.

Most importantly, don't be afraid to try new ideas, and don't feel like you have to be an expert. You just need to start with *one thing* in your classroom or school and then take time to evaluate the impact. Involve students in the conversations and then decide upon next steps. We are always learning, evaluating, reflecting, and setting new goals as educators. With AI, we simply need to continue to do the same.

As you seek to provide the best learning experiences to prepare your students, reflect on the choices you make in your classroom. What are the benefits for students? What are the benefits for your professional work and growth? Consider the ISTE Standards that we have covered throughout the book. How will you address the standards in your classroom and in your professional practice?

Keeping a clear focus on the benefits of technology in preparing our students to be successful in the future is essential. What can we do as Leaders, Learners, Designers, and Facilitators that helps our students to become Empowered Learners, Digital Citizens, Innovative Designers, Knowledge Constructors, and Creative Communicators? Having goals in mind will help us all to best navigate the changing world of education and, in particular, the changing world when it comes to AI.

Share your ideas with me on X (formerly Twitter) @Rdene915 or post a message on LinkedIn. I look forward to hearing about your AI journey and discoveries.

Appendix A

Sample Lesson Ideas for All Levels

In this appendix you will find sample activities and lesson plans to try in the classroom. Activities are arranged by ascending grade levels. In addition, I've provided an example of drafting and refining a lesson plan using a generative AI tool.

⧉ Activity 1: Exploring AI with Chatbots

Grade level: Elementary school

Objective: To introduce elementary school students to the concept of AI and chatbots and to encourage them to think about how chatbots work.

Discussion questions:

✦ How would you describe what AI is?

✦ What are some examples of AI in daily life?

✦ Have you ever used a chatbot? Have you seen a customer service chat on a website?

✦ How do you think chatbots are able to understand and provide responses to questions?

✦ Name some benefits of using chatbots.

Project idea: Have students create a chatbot using a platform like Scratch (**scratch.mit.edu**) or other age-appropriate chatbot-building tool. The students can program the chatbot to answer questions that are focused on a specific topic, such as animals, history, or their favorite books.

⧉ Activity 2: Introduction to AI and Robots

Grade level: Elementary school

Objective: To introduce elementary school students to the concept of AI and robots.

Discussion questions:

✦ What is AI, and what do you know about robots?

✦ What are some things robots can do?

✦ What are some ways that robots could be helpful to people?

✦ What is something that a human could do that a robot could not?

Project idea: Ask students to draw and describe their own imaginary robot and explain its purpose and special features. An activity like this is a great way to encourage creativity and spark curiosity for learning and engage students in collaborative learning.

ⵣ Activity 3: Ethics of AI in Decision-Making

Grade level: Middle school

Objective: To introduce middle school students to the importance of ethical considerations related to AI.

Discussion questions:

✦ What is artificial intelligence, and how does it make decisions?

✦ What are some examples of when AI is used to make decisions in society (e.g., algorithms that make recommendations such as Amazon, self-driving cars)?

✦ Can you think of some ethical concerns related to AI decision-making?

✦ How can we ensure that AI systems make fair and unbiased decisions?

Project idea: An opportunity to help students develop critical-thinking skills and collaboration would be to have them work with a partner or in a small group. Have students research and analyze a real-world case where AI decision-making led to ethical concerns. Once they complete their research and discuss, they can share with classmates and propose solutions for how to address the ethical issues.

ⵣ Activity 4: AI in Healthcare and Ethical Considerations

Grade level: High school

Objective: To educate high school students about the applications of AI in healthcare and consider potential ethical issues.

Discussion questions:

✦ How is AI used in the field of healthcare?

✦ What are the potential benefits of using AI in diagnosing diseases and providing medical treatment? What are the benefits of using chatbots in healthcare?

✦ What are the ethical concerns that might arise when AI is used in healthcare?

- How can we ensure the ethical and responsible use of AI in healthcare?
- Look for news articles discussing the use of AI in healthcare and share with the class. See what questions and concerns come up from classmates.

Project idea: Assign students to research and present on a specific application of AI in healthcare (e.g., medical imaging, drug discovery, therapy services). They should find out if and how AI is being used, as well as look for any ethical considerations. Students could select from a list of healthcare topics and then share with classmates. An extension would be to have students create their own application of AI for healthcare.

✦ Activity 5: AI and Machine Learning in Data Analysis

Grade level: High school

Objective: To teach high school students the basics of AI and machine learning and advance to more complex functions such as analyzing data and algorithms.

Discussion questions:

- What is the difference between AI and machine learning?
- How are AI and machine learning used in data analysis and predictions?
- Can you find examples of machine-learning algorithms and how they work?
- What are the challenges and ethical considerations when using AI for data analysis?

Project idea: Assign students to learn about natural language processing (NLP) or AI and how it is used for predictive analytics in different jobs. Students can then share their findings and engage in discussions with classmates about the benefits and any ethical concerns.

✦ Activity 6: AI and Robotics in Automation

Grade level: High school (advanced)

Objective: To provide high school students with an understanding of AI and robotics in automation, and consider the potential impact on the future of work.

Discussion questions:

✦ What is automation, and how does AI play a role in it?

✦ Can you think of industries where automation and robotics are used?

✦ What are the benefits and drawbacks of this technology?

✦ How do robots use AI to perform tasks, and what are the benefits?

✦ What are the potential impacts of automation on the job market and society?

Project idea: Challenge students to design an automated system using robotics and AI. The topic can be related to the content area or an area of interest. Students should present their project and explain its benefits and potential negatives. Engage students in a class discussion to extend the learning experience and generate new ideas.

Workflow for Creating a Lesson Plan with Generative AI

Using ChatGPT to generate ideas or to provide differentiation can be very efficient. Here are some examples of prompts and the plans ChatGPT generated from them during a typical AI-assisted lesson plan creation session.

Enter a Prompt

I began with a detailed prompt (**Figure A.1**):

Your role is as a sixth-grade teacher who wants to have students write a persuasive essay based on topics related to the use of artificial intelligence. Write a total of six lesson overviews with objectives, timeline, relevant standards, requirements, discussion questions, and create a rubric for each of these. Three of the lessons should have students in favor of and three against the use of AI.

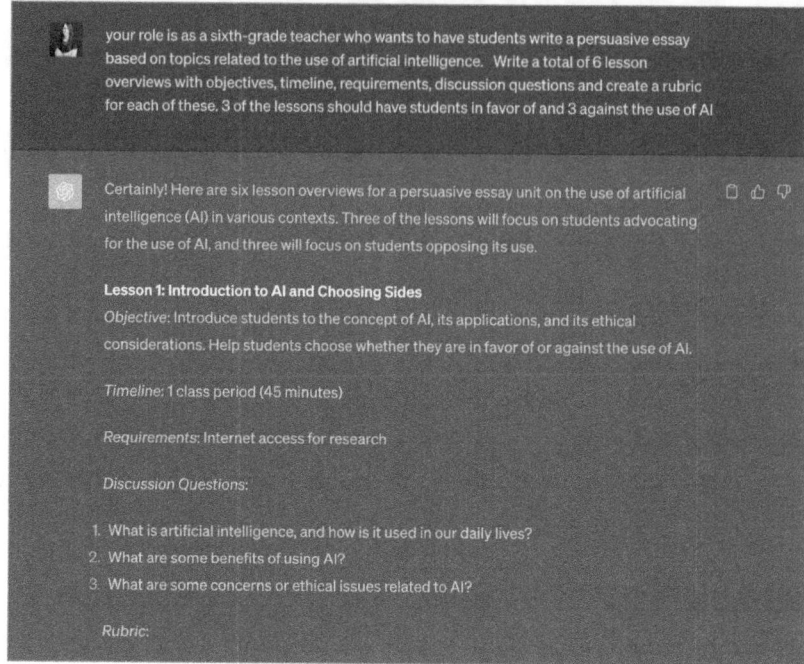

Response: Lesson 1: Introduction to AI and Choosing Sides

Objective: Introduce students to the concept of AI, its applications, and its ethical considerations. Help students choose whether they are in favor of or against the use of AI.

Timeline: 1 class period (45 minutes)

Requirements: Internet access for research

Discussion questions:

✦ What is artificial intelligence, and how is it used in our daily lives?

✦ What are some benefits of using AI?

✦ What are some concerns or ethical issues related to AI?

Rubric:

✦ Participation in class discussion (10 points)

✦ Clarity of chosen stance (10 points)

✦ Identification of one reason for their chosen stance (10 points)

Enter a Follow-Up Prompt (Optional)

The first prompt provided a rubric in the list form only, which was not sufficient for using with the lesson, so I entered a new prompt:

Create a rubric for 2 of the lessons.

ChatGPT then returned the rubric in a chart shown in **Figure A.2**.

FIGURE A.2
Prompting ChatGPT to
develop a rubric to be
used for the lessons

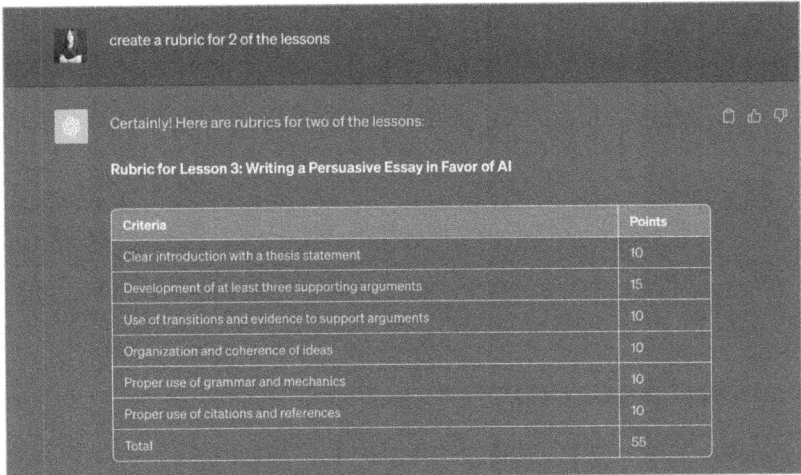

Request Revisions and Elaborations

I wanted more details for the lessons, so I requested a revision with the prompt:

Revise each lesson and expand the details for the lesson to provide short definitions, activities for students to collaborate and project extensions.

ChatGPT: Sure, let's revise and expand each lesson with short definitions, collaborative activities, and project extensions.

After this response, the program generated the more detailed lessons shown in the sections below.

Lesson 1: Introduction to AI and Choosing Sides

Objective: Introduce students to the concept of AI, its applications, and its ethical considerations. Help students choose whether they are in favor of or against the use of AI.

Timeline: 1 class period (45 minutes)

Short definitions:

✦ **Artificial intelligence (AI):** A technology that enables computers and machines to perform tasks that typically require human intelligence, such as learning, problem-solving, and decision-making.

Activities for collaboration:

✦ **AI Showcase:** In small groups, students research and present examples of AI applications in everyday life, discussing both the benefits and potential concerns.

✦ **Debate Prep:** Students form pairs and engage in a mini-debate, taking on the roles of pro-AI and anti-AI advocates, to practice argumentation.

Project extension: For homework, students write a brief reflection on their chosen stance, citing one reason and one concern related to AI.

Lesson 2: Researching Arguments in Favor of AI

Objective: Encourage students to explore the positive aspects and potential benefits of AI.

Timeline: 2 class periods (90 minutes total)

Short definitions:

✦ **Machine learning:** A subset of AI that allows computers to improve their performance on a task through experience and data.

Activities for collaboration:

✦ **AI Impact Analysis:** In groups, students research and analyze how AI has positively impacted specific industries (e.g., healthcare, transportation), identifying key benefits and presenting their findings.

✦ **AI in the Future:** As a class, discuss the potential future applications of AI, and have students work together to brainstorm and present innovative ideas.

Project extension: Students create a visual timeline or infographic highlighting the historical milestones of AI development.

Lesson 3: Writing a Persuasive Essay in Favor of AI

Objective: Teach students the structure of a persuasive essay and guide them in drafting the introduction and body paragraphs supporting their pro-AI stance.

Timeline: 2 class periods (90 minutes total)

Short definitions:

✦ **Persuasive essay:** A type of writing that aims to convince the reader to adopt a particular viewpoint or take a specific action.

Activities for collaboration:

✦ **Thesis Workshop:** Students work in pairs to develop clear thesis statements supporting AI, providing constructive feedback to refine their statements.

✦ **Peer Review:** Exchange essays with a partner, review each other's introductions, and offer suggestions for improvement.

Project extension: Incorporate a visual element, such as creating an accompanying poster or infographic to enhance the persuasive power of their essays.

Lesson 4: Researching Arguments Against AI

Objective: Encourage students to explore the negative aspects and potential risks of AI.

Timeline: 2 class periods (90 minutes total)

Short definitions:

✦ **Ethical concerns:** Moral issues and dilemmas associated with the use of technology, including AI.

Activities for collaboration:

✦ **AI Ethics Panel:** In groups, students research and role-play an ethics panel discussion, debating ethical concerns related to AI (e.g., privacy, job displacement).

✦ **Case Studies:** Analyze and discuss real-world examples of AI misuse or unintended consequences as a class, identifying key lessons learned.

Project extension: Students create a "Code of Ethics" for AI developers, outlining principles to guide responsible AI development and usage.

Evaluate the Results

Notice that the revised lessons provide more detailed definitions, collaborative activities, and project extensions to engage sixth-grade students in exploring AI from multiple perspectives while enhancing their critical-thinking and research skills. You could also consider providing the length of class periods, asking for specific standards to be included, or requesting a more detailed overview of each lesson.

Appendix B

Resources

This appendix offers AI-related resources for educators—from articles, books, and podcasts to ready-to-run presentations, tools, and videos to organizations that offer full AI curriculums. You'll find insight into the use of AI, skills in demand, ways to bring AI into the classroom, and more. Wondering where to start? For research, my advice is to look to publications from ISTE and Getting Smart for a few examples. For tools, dive in and try things. Remember, though, that some of the listed tools fit into multiple categories because of the robust platform or resources they offer.

Keep in mind, as well, that this list is just a snapshot in time of what's available. As I find more resources and test new tools, I will update the book's online resources list. Scan the QR code to check it out.

tinyurl.com/ykt7c8z9

Books, Articles, and More to Read

✦ "10 Best AI Tools for Education" by Alex McFarland (**unite.ai/10-best-ai-tools-for-education**)

✦ "The 10 Best Examples of How AI Is Already Used in Our Everyday Lives" by Bernard Marr (**bit.ly/3UbMZpN**)

✦ "18 In-Demand Technology Skills to Learn in 2022," article from *Learn to Code with Me* (**learntocodewith.me/posts/tech-skills-in-demand**)

✦ "50 ChatGPT Prompts for Teachers," article from TeacherMade (**teachermade.com/50-chatgpt-prompts-for-teachers**)

✦ "50 ChatGPT Prompts for Teachers" by Marcee Harris (**teachingchannel.com/k12-hub/blog/50-chat-gpt-prompts-for-teachers**)

✦ *AI in Education*, whitepaper from GettingSmart (**gettingsmart.com/categories/topics/artificial-intelligence**)

✦ *AITopics*, article collection from Association for the Advancement of Artificial Intelligence (**aitopics.org/search**)

✦ *Artificial Intelligence in Education* by Wayne Holmes, Maya Bialik, and Charles Fadel (**amazon.com/Artificial-Intelligence-Education-Promises-Implications/dp/1794293701**)

✦ "Artificial Intelligence: An Explainer for Beginners" by Nishant Sirohi (**theleaflet.in/artificial-intelligence-an-explainer-for-beginners**)

✦ "Five Jobs that Artificial Intelligence Will Replace in the Future," article from Analytics Insight (**analyticsinsight.net/five-jobs-that-artificial-intelligence-will-replace-in-future**)

✦ "How to Use ChatGPT like a Pro: 100+ Examples for Teachers with Prompts You Can Copy" by Zhun Yee Chew (**classpoint.io/blog/how-to-use-chatgpt-100-chatgpt-examples-in-schools**)

✦ Teacher and Student Guide to Analyzing AI Writing Tools, online guide from EdTech Books (**edtechbooks.org/mediaandciviclearning/cmlguides#h2_xqej**)

✦ "Top 10 Low-Cost AI Projects for Your Kids to Work on" by Aishwarya Banik (**analyticsinsight.net/top-10-low-cost-ai-projects-for-your-kids-to-work-on**)

Organizations Offering AI Resources for Educators

✦ **AI4ALL** (ai-4-all.org/resources) offers an Open Learning Curriculum on AI. There are a variety of lessons, including AI & Art, AI & Dance, AI & Ethics, How Neural Networks Work, and more. All include teaching guides, full slideshows with questions, objectives, and videos (**Figure B.1**).

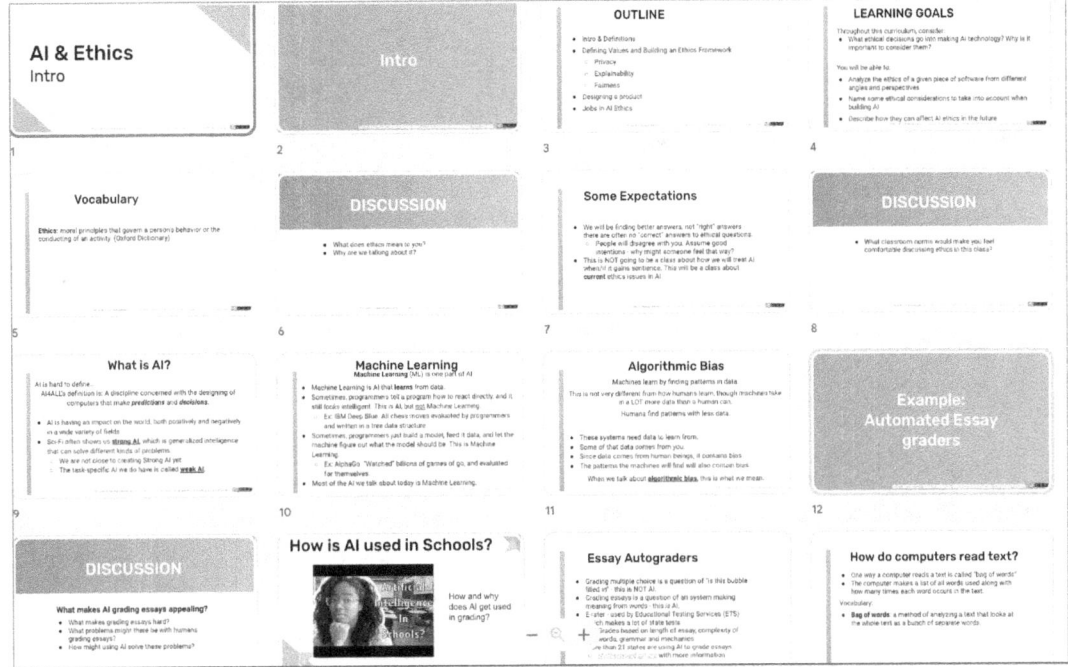

FIGURE B.1
AI4ALL offers presentations for classroom use, complete with slides, videos embedded, discussion questions, and other teaching materials.

✦ **AI4K12** offers a curated list of resources (ai4k12.org/resources/list-of-resources), activities for students (ai4k12.org/activities), teaching aids and posters (ai4k12.org/gradeband-progression-charts), and more. Educators can find plenty of information about activities for bringing AI into K–12 classrooms.

✦ **AIClub** (aiclub.world/about) offers a wealth of activities for students of all ages, as well as books, online courses, PD, and resources for educators. For elementary students, AIClub Gym (**my.aiclub.world/ai_gym**) offers fun activities for elementary students (**Figure B.2**), plus AIClub has videos, activities, and other materials for students in grades 5–8 (**corp.aiclub.world/fun-ai-activities-grades5-8**). For extended learning, students can explore the AIClub projects available (**my.aiclub.world/projects?tab=projects**). There are even projects that help students to understand the use of AI in healthcare (**corp.aiclub.world/post/ai-medicine-healthcare-projects-for-kids**).

FIGURE B.2
AIClub Gym provides activities that help elementary students explore AI in relation to different content areas.

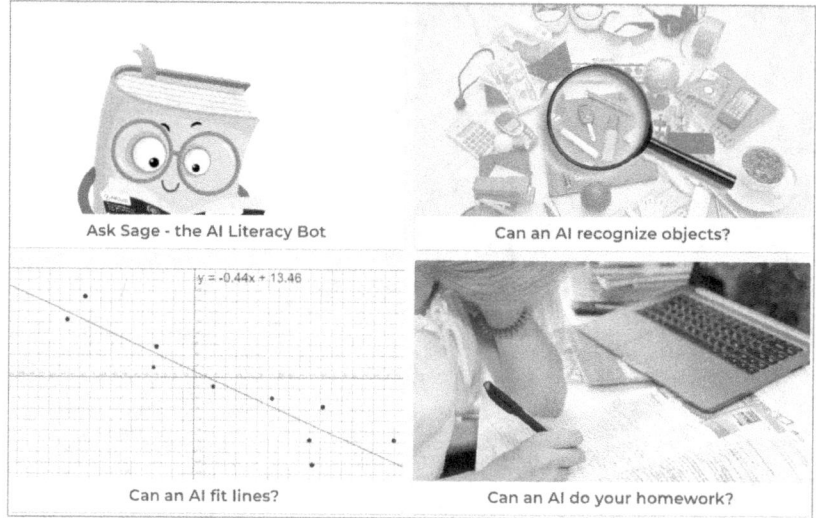

Ask Sage - the AI Literacy Bot

Can an AI recognize objects?

$y = -0.44x + 13.46$

Can an AI fit lines?

Can an AI do your homework?

+ **AI for Teachers** (**aiforteachers.org**) is full of activities to help you learn how to bring artificial intelligence into your classroom. It provides lessons for students in grades K–5, 6–8, and 9–12 that progressively expand the complexity of activities that the students are engaging in with each grade band. Some of the topics include bias and ethics, autonomous vehicles, and more.

+ **AI World School** (**aiworldschool.com**) offers independent learning as well as teacher-led courses and activities for three age bands, including a Virtual Driverless Car course for students aged 14 and over. There are also activities available for students to explore in the Play AI for Free section.

+ **aiEDU** (**aiedu.org**) hosts the AI Education Project, which offers online lessons and challenges for students and educators as well as classroom curricula.

+ **Coursera** (**coursera.org/learn/artificial-intelligence-education-for-teachers**) offers a free AI for Educators course for beginners. Available in nineteen languages, the course takes approximately sixteen hours to complete. The site also offers courses specific to ChatGPT, generative AI, and more advanced topics.

- ✦ **Day of AI** (dayofai.org) was developed by MIT RAISE (Responsible AI for Social Empowerment and Education) and provides curriculum focused on AI for students in grades K–12. Topics include fundamentals of AI and its impact on society. Each year, schools can participate in the "Day of AI," which has activities available across four grade bands. There is also a focus on careers in AI.

- ✦ **edX** (edx.org/learn/artificial-intelligence) offers a variety of courses focused on AI and also provides information related to obtaining degrees and certification in artificial intelligence.

- ✦ **Facing History** (facinghistory.org/resource-library/ethics-generative-ai-classroom) offers mini-lessons for students in grades 6–12 on generative AI tools, such as ChatGPT and DALL•E, and lessons focused on ethical considerations.

- ✦ **Google** partnered with the Oxford Internet Institute to create The A to Z of AI (emea.brandstudio.goog/a-z-of-ai). There are topics related to AI (alphabetized from A to Z) explained in detail to help educators and students gain a better understanding of key terms. Google also offers ready-made activities to use in the classroom (experiments.withgoogle.com/experiments). For educators getting started, the Experiments with Google and Labs.Google offer easy ways to have students explore AI and activities that help them to learn about aspects of AI, such as neural networks.

- ✦ **ISTE** (iste.org/ai) offers a school leaders guide to AI, *Hands-On AI Projects for the Classroom* guides for various grade levels and content specialties, a guide on ethics and AI, as well as educator courses on AI via ISTE U.

- ✦ **Khan Academy** (khanacademy.org/college-careers-more/ai-for-education) offers a three-unit course for educators to learn about generative AI and how to teach with AI. It includes lesson plans from Common Sense Education with topics such as bias, chatbots, facial recognition, and algorithms.

- ✦ **Microsoft Educator Center** (learn.microsoft.com/en-us/training/educator-center/?source=mec) offers a wide range of free professional development courses, lesson plans, teaching materials, and tutorials available for educators to explore.

- ✦ **MIT** (thecenter.mit.edu/wp-content/uploads/2020/07/MIT-AI-Ethics-Education-Curriculum.pdf) offers an AI and Ethics curriculum in multiple languages. Each of the activities is aligned with the ISTE Student Standards.

- ✦ **RAISE** (Responsible AI for Social Empowerment and Education) offers the MIT AI Literacy Units (raise.mit.edu/resources). Each unit comes with information, student activities, and even curriculum. You can also find professional development resources for educators.

- **TeachAI** offers an AI Guidance for Schools Toolkit in conjunction with the ISTE (**teachai.org/toolkit**), which was developed in conjunction with **code.org**, ETS, Khan Academy, and ISTE.

- **Udemy** (**udemy.com/course/ai-for-teachers-and-educators**) offers an introductory AI course called AI for Teachers and Educators. The course covers what AI is, key technologies, ethics, and tips for using AI in the classroom.

- **United States Department of Education Office of Educational Technology (OET)** published *Artificial Intelligence and the Future of Teaching & Learning* (**www2.ed.gov/documents/ai-report/ai-report.pdf**), which includes recommendations for educators to help with bringing AI learning opportunities into the classrooms, sample activities, and more. Also available are videos discussing policies that are needed, blog posts on AI, and a call to action for education leaders (**tech.ed.gov/ai**).

Podcasts

- "10 Best AI in Education Podcasts for Students and Educators" by Oliver Bugarin (**bcast.fm/blog/best-ai-in-education-podcasts**)

- "The 11 Best AI & Machine Learning Podcasts to Add to Your Listening Pipeline" by Olivia Lengyel (**blog.paperspace.com/11-best-ai-and-machine-learning-podcasts**)

- "22 AI Podcasts Worth a Listen" by Lisa Bertagnoli (**builtin.com/artificial-intelligence/ai-podcast**)

- *The EdTech Bites Podcast* (**edtechbites.libsyn.com/ep-184-the-ai-evolution-in-education-rachelle-den-poths-top-3-picks-for-ai-in-education**)

- *Learning Unleashed:* "How Exploring AI with Students Can Reduce Stress and Open New Possibilities" (**bamradionetwork.com/track/how-exploring-ai-with-students-can-reduces-stress-and-open-new-possibilities**)

- *MIT Computer Science and Artificial Intelligence Lab Alliances Podcast:* "How AI Will Shape the Future of Education" (**cap.csail.mit.edu/podcasts/how-ai-will-shape-future-education-hal-abelson**)

- *OnEdMentors Podcast:* "ChatGPT and AI in EDU" (**voiced.ca/podcast_episode_post/chatgpt-and-ai-in-edu**)

- *ThriveinEDU Podcast* (**podcasters.spotify.com/pod/show/rdene915**)

Tools for Teachers
Assessments, Clerical Tasks, Lesson Planning, Presentations

- ✦ Almanack (almanack.ai)
- ✦ Brisk Teaching (briskteaching.com)
- ✦ Conker (conker.ai)
- ✦ Curipod (curipod.com)
- ✦ Diffit (beta.diffit.me/#topic)
- ✦ Eduaide.Ai (eduaide.ai)
- ✦ Education Copilot (educationcopilot.com)
- ✦ EnlightenAI (enlightenme.ai)
- ✦ Flint (flintk12.com)
- ✦ Formative (app.formative.com)
- ✦ fobizz AI (fobizz.com; **Figure B.3**)
- ✦ Khanmigo (khanmigo.ai)

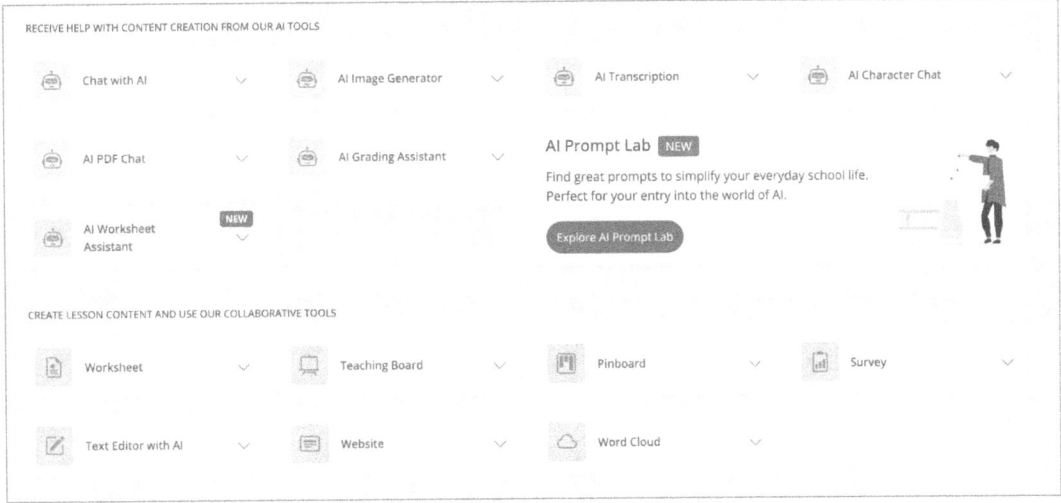

FIGURE B.3
fobizz offers a variety of tools to help educators create class resources and a safe space for students to interact with AI.

- Knewton (**knewton.com**)
- Learnt.ai (**learnt.ai/how-it-works?ref=aieducator.tools**)
- LessonPlans.AI (**lessonplans.ai**)
- MagicSchool AI (**magicschool.ai**)
- Microsoft Copilot (**copilot.microsoft.com**; **Figure B.4**)

FIGURE B.4
Copilot is an AI companion that can help to generate ideas. It also provides Copilot GPTs on several topics.

- Padlet/Magic Padlet (**padlet.com**; **padlet.help/l/en/article/w9yl61m88g-magic-padlet**)
- QuestionWell (**questionwell.org**)
- Quizizz (**quizizz.com**)
- Quizlet (**quizlet.com**)
- Schemely (**schemely.app**)
- SchoolAI (**schoolai.com**)
- Slidesgo (**slidesgo.com**)
- SlidesPilot (**slidespilot.com**)
- Snorkl (**go.snorkl.app/rachelle**; **Figures B.5** and **B.6**)

FIGURE B.5

Students provide responses using Snorkl, then teachers can scroll through, see, and hear the responses as well as provide feedback.

FIGURE B.6

Snorkl provides AI-generated feedback with time stamps.

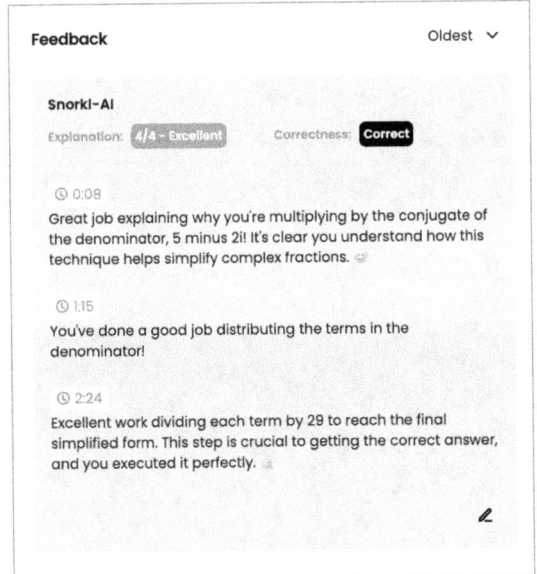

- There's an AI for That (**theresanaiforthat.com**)
- Tome (**tome.app**)
- Twee (**twee.com**)
- Wepik (**wepik.com**)

Chatbot Creation and Exploration

- AI4K12 Chatbot with BERT (**ai4k12.org/wp-content/uploads/2023/04/ Chatbot-with-BERT-Activity-Guide-1.pdf**)
- Amazon Lex Chatbot (**aws.amazon.com/lex**)
- Appy Pie Chatbot (**appypie.com/chatbot/builder**)
- Chat for Schools (**chatforschools.com**)
- Dante AI (**dante-ai.com**)
- ISTE StretchAI Chatbot (**iste.org/ai**)
- MIT App Inventor (**appinventor.mit.edu**)
- Poe (**poe.com**)
- SkoolOfCode: Build a Chatbot (**skoolofcode.us/blog/ how-to-make-a-chatbot-for-kids-using-machine-learning**)
- Zapier (**zapier.com/ai/chatbot**)

Devices

- AutoAuto (**autoauto.ai**)
- KinderLab Robotics KIBO (**kinderlabrobotics.com/resources/activities**)
- Marty the Robot (**robotical.io/about/all-about-marty**)
- MatataStudio (**matatalab.com**)
- PASCO Coding with Vehicle Sensor Technologies Kit (**pasco.com/products/ stem-sense/coding-with-sensors/st-7820**)
- PCEye (**us.tobiidynavox.com/pages/pceye**)

Generative AI

✦ Adobe Firefly (**adobe.com/products/firefly.html**; **Figure B.7**)

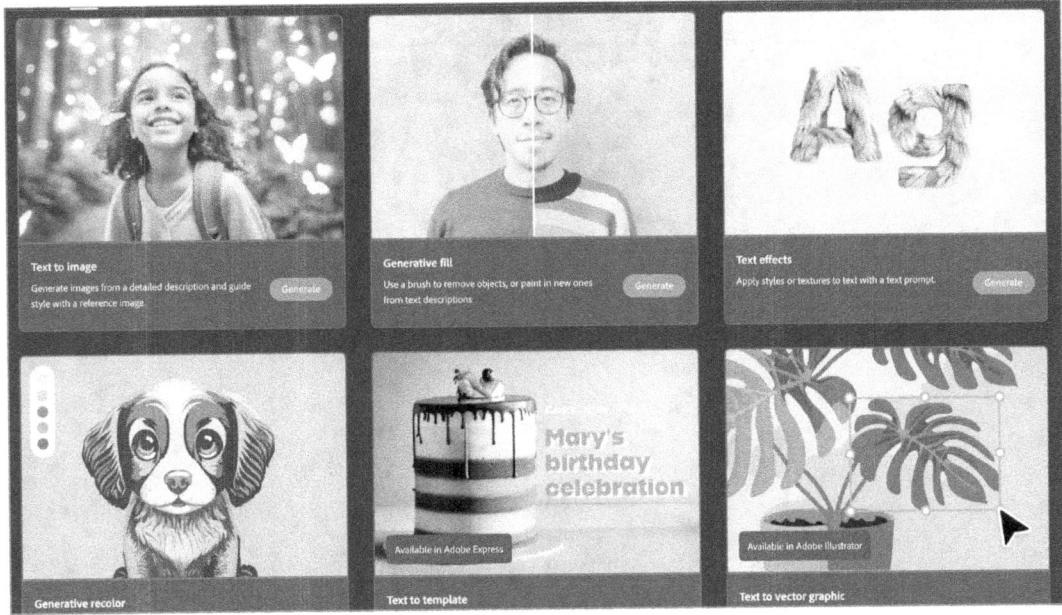

FIGURE B.7
Adobe Firefly can generate various types of media from a prompt and offers many AI features for working with images, such as Text to Image, Generative Fill, and Generative Recolor.

✦ Canva (**canva.com**)

✦ ChatGPT/ChatGPT Plus (**openai.com/chatgpt**)

✦ Claude (**anthropic.com/claude**)

✦ Copilot (**copilot.microsoft.com**)

✦ Craiyon (**craiyon.com**; **Figure B.8**)

FIGURE B.8
With Craiyon, enter a prompt to generate an image. Once the images are generated, Craiyon offers an additional prompt idea to generate new images.

- DALL•E 3 (**openai.com/dall-e-3**)
- D-ID (**d-id.com**)
- Genie (**lumalabs.ai/genie**)
- Google Gemini (**gemini.google.com/app**)
- Microsoft Designer (**designer.microsoft.com/home**)
- Microsoft Seeing AI (**microsoft.com/en-us/ai/seeing-ai**)
- Midjourney (**midjourney.com**)
- OpenArt (**openart.ai/create**)
- Parlay Genie (**new.parlayideas.com**)
- Perplexity (**perplexity.ai**)
- PIXLR (**pixlr.com/image-generator**; **Figure B.9**)

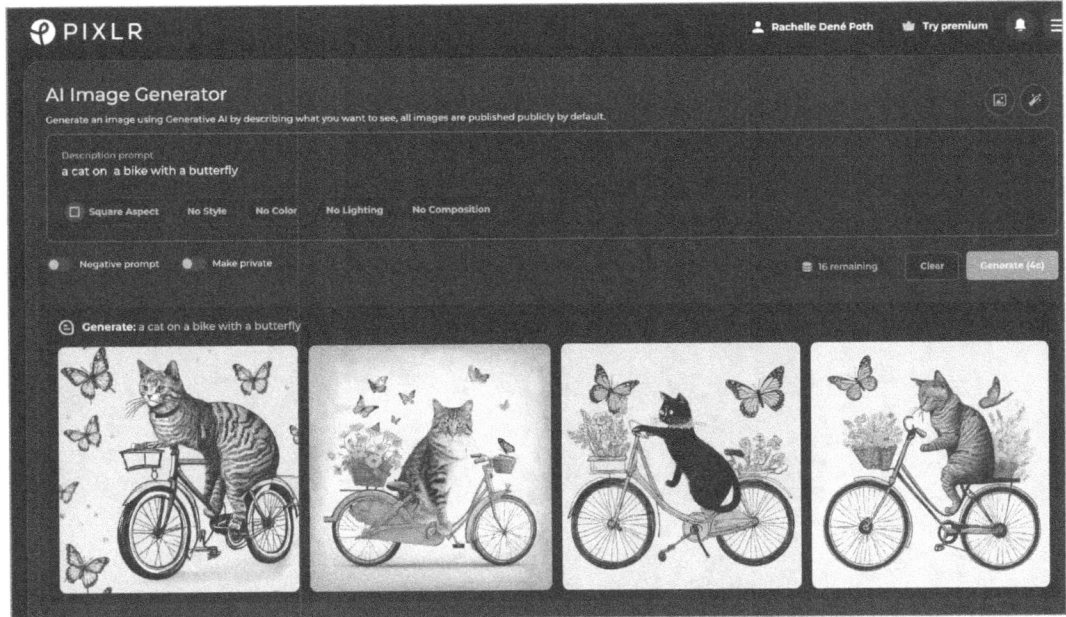

FIGURE B.9
You enter descriptive text and select a style, and PIXLR generates an image. If you don't want the result added to the public image library, click Make Private.

- ✦ Quick, Draw! (**quickdraw.withgoogle.com**)
- ✦ Stable Audio (**stableaudio.com**)
- ✦ Synthesia (**synthesia.io**)
- ✦ Verse by Verse (**sites.research.google/versebyverse**)
- ✦ Wombo Dream (**wombo.art**)
- ✦ YouChat (**web.youchat.com**)

Research, Writing, or Differentiation

- ✦ Class Companion (**classcompanion.com**)
- ✦ Elicit (**elicit.com**)
- ✦ Goblin Tools (**goblin.tools**)
- ✦ Grammarly (**grammarly.com**)

- Microsoft Immersive Reader (**bit.ly/MLECenter**)
- Newsela (**newsela.com**)
- Otter (**otter.ai**)
- Passed.AI (**passed.ai**)
- PowerNotes (**powernotes.com**)
- Prodigy Math (**prodigygame.com**)
- Quillbot (**quillbot.com**)
- Sorcerer (**antimatter.systems/sorcerer**)
- TutorAI (**tutorai.me**)
- Will Robots Take My Job? (**willrobotstakemyjob.com**)

Speech and Translation

- AudioPen (**audiopen.ai**)
- Dragon Speech Recognition Solutions (**nuance.com/dragon.html**)
- Duolingo (**duolingo.com**)
- Google Translate (**translate.google.com**)
- Knowji (**knowji.com**)
- Speechify (**studio.speechify.com**; **Figure B.10**)
- TalkPal AI (**talkpal.ai**)

FIGURE B.10
To generate a voiceover using Speechify, add text or import a script, and then choose a speaking tone.

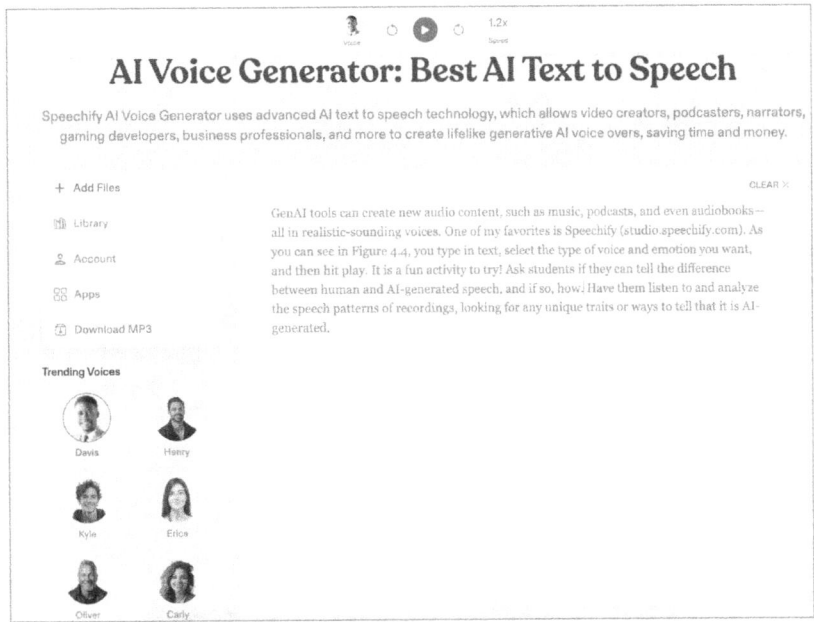

Student Activities

✦ Akinator (akinator.com)

✦ CareerDekho (careerdekho.ai)

✦ DreamBox Math and DreamBox Reading (dreambox.com)

✦ Elements of AI (elementsofai.com)

✦ Google AI Experiments (experiments.withgoogle.com/experiments)

✦ Hello History (hellohistory.ai)

✦ Human vs AI Test (tidio.com/blog/ai-test)

✦ Interviews by AI (interviewsby.ai)

✦ Intro to Artificial Intelligence Bootcamps (markcubanai.org)

✦ Moral Machine (moralmachine.net)

✦ Python & AI with Autonomous Cars (labs.autoauto.ai/shop/aa_courses)

✦ ReadyAI (readyai.org)

✦ Say What You See (artsandculture.google.com/experiment/jwG3m7wQShZngw)

- SchoolAI (**schoolai.com**)
- Semantris (**experiments.withgoogle.com/semantris**)
- Virtual Driverless Car (**aiworldschool.com/product/virtual-driverless-car**)

Videos

- C.L.Ai.R.A. (**youtube.com/watch?v=dieN9KymmPc**)
- Crash Course AI (**youtube.com/watch?v=a0_lo_GDcFw**)
- Generative AI Is About to Reset Everything, and, Yes It Will Change Your Life (**youtube.com/watch?v=WY518YRfs5M**)
- How Will AI Change the World? (**youtube.com/watch?v=RzkD_rTEBYs**)
- Is Atlas the World's Most Advanced Humanoid Robot with Artificial Intelligence Until Now? (**youtu.be/yBdyU1JCpwg**)
- What Is AI? Artificial Intelligence Facts for Kids (**youtube.com/watch?v=pv9GF281Dp0**)
- What Is Artificial Intelligence? (**youtu.be/nASDYRkbQIY**)
- Teach AI: Prepare Our Students for the Future (**youtube.com/watch?v=YmZJmmys7Ps**)

References

Abdelmohsen, E. (2023, May 26). Navigating the future of autonomous vehicles. *Infomineo*. https://infomineo.com/industrial-goods/navigating-the-future-of-autonomous-vehicles

Abdulkader, A., Lakshimiratan, A., & Zhang, J. (2016, June 1). Introducing DeepText: Facebook's text understanding engine. *Engineering at Meta*. https://code.facebook.com/posts/181565595577955/introducing-deeptext-facebook-s-text-understanding-engine

Adobe. (2024a). *Adobe Firefly*. https://www.adobe.com/products/firefly.html

Adobe. (2024b). *AI at Adobe*. https://www.adobe.com/about-adobe/aiethics.html

Akgun, S., & Greenhow, C. (2022, August). Artificial intelligence in education: Addressing ethical challenges in k–12 settings. *AI Ethics*, 2(3), 431–440. https://doi.org/10.1007/s43681-021-00096-7

American Civil Liberties Union. (2022, May 9). *In big win, settlement ensures Clearview AI complies with groundbreaking Illinois biometric privacy law*. https://www.aclu.org/press-releases/big-win-settlement-ensures-clearview-ai-complies-with-groundbreaking-illinois

Axios. (2019, January 10). *AI expert warns automation could take 40% of jobs by 2035*. https://www.axios.com/2019/01/10/artificial-intelligence-automation-jobs-robots

Bhuiyan, J. (2023, December 20). Rite Aid facial recognition misidentified Black, Latino and Asian people as "likely" shoplifters. *The Guardian*. https://www.theguardian.com/technology/2023/dec/20/rite-aid-shoplifting-facial-recognition-ftc-settlement

Bryant, J., Heitz, C., Sanghvi, S., & Wagle, D. (2020, January 14). How artificial intelligence will impact k–12 teachers. *McKinsey & Company*. https://www.mckinsey.com/inddustries/education/our-insights/how-artificial-intelligence-will-impact-k-12-teachers

Cao, L., & Dede, C. (2023). *Navigating a world of generative AI: Suggestions for educators*. The Next Level Lab at Harvard Graduate School of Education. President and Fellows of Harvard College. https://nextlevellab.gse.harvard.edu/2023/07/28/navigating-a-world-of-generative-ai-suggestions-for-educators

Celik, I. (2023, January). Towards intelligent-TPACK: An empirical study on teachers' professional knowledge to ethically integrate artificial intelligence (AI)-based tools into education. *Computers in Human Behavior*, 138, 107468. https://doi.org/10.1016/j.chb.2022.107468

Channa, F. R., Sarhandi, P. S. A., Bugti, F., & Pathan, H. (2021). Harnessing artificial intelligence in education for preparing learners for the 21st century. *Elementary Education Online*, 20(5), 3186–3192. https://www.academia.edu/45647427/Harnessing_Artificial_Intelligence_in_Education_for_Preparing_Learners_for_the_21st_Century_Harnessing_Artificial_Intelligence_in_Education_for_Preparing_Learners_for_the_21st_Century

Create Labs. (2023). *Meet C.L.Ai.R.A.* https://createlabs.io/claira

Crompton, H., & Burke, D., (2022). Artificial intelligence in k–12 education. *SN Social Sciences*, 2(7), 113. https://doi.org/10.1007/s43545-022-00425-5

Crompton, H., Jones, M. V., & Burke, D. (2022, September 13). Affordances and challenges of artificial intelligence in k–12 education: A systematic review. *Journal of Research on Technology in Education*. https://doi.org/10.1080/15391523.2022.2121344

Dartmouth College. (2023). *Artificial intelligence coined at Dartmouth.* https://home.dartmouth.edu/about/artificial-intelligence-ai-coined-dartmouth

David, E. (2023, December 4). Getty lawsuit against Stability AI to go to trial in.the UK. *The Verge.* https://www.theverge.com/2023/12/4/23988403/getty-lawsuit-stability-ai-copyright-infringement

Domínguez, A. (2023, March 22). We can't keep ChatGPT out of the classroom, so let's address the "why" behind our fears. *EdSurge.* https://www.edsurge.com/news/2023-03-22-we-can-t-keep-chatgpt-out-of-the-classroom-so-let-s-address-the-why-behind-our-fears

Duffy, C., & Goldman, D. (2023, December 27). The *New York Times* sues OpenAI and Microsoft for copyright infringement. *CNN.* https://www.cnn.com/2023/12/27/tech/new-york-times-sues-openai-microsoft/index.html

Edison & Black (2023, May 12). *Over 97 million jobs set to be created by AI.* https://edisonandblack.com/pages/over-97-million-jobs-set-to-be-created-by-ai.html

Eke, D. O. (2023, April). ChatGPT and the rise of generative AI: Threat to academic integrity? *Journal of Responsible Technology*, 13, 100060. https://doi.org/10.1016/j.jrt.2023.100060

Ellingrud, K., Sanghvi, S., Dandona, G. S., Madgavkar, A., Chui, M., White, O., & Hasebe, P. (2023, July 26). Generative AI and the future of work in America. *McKinsey Global Institute.* https://www.mckinsey.com/mgi/our-research/generative-ai-and-the-future-of-work-in-america

Feger, A. (2023, April 19). AI spending will jump to $154 billion worldwide in 2023. *Insider Intelligence.* https://www.insiderintelligence.com/content/ai-spending-will-jump-billion-worldwide-2023

Getting Smart. (2018). *AI in education.* https://www.gettingsmart.com/whitepaper/artificial-intelligence

Gill, S. S, Xu, M., Patros, P., Wu, H., Kaur, R., Kaur, K., Fuller, S., Singh, M., Arora, P., Parlikad, A. K., Stankovski, V., Abraham, A., Ghosh, S. K., Lutfiyya, H., Kanhere, S. S., Bahsoon, R., Rana, O., Dustdar, S., Sakellariou, R., Uhlig, S., & Buyya, R. (2024). Transformative effects of ChatGPT on modern education: Emerging era of AI chatbots. *Internet of Things and Cyber-Physical Systems*, 4(2024), 19–23. https://doi.org/10.1016/j.iotcps.2023.06.002

GlobeNewswire. (2023, April 6). *AI in education market size to reach USD 23.82 billion by 2030 with a CAGR of 38%—report by Market Research Future (MRFR).* https://www.globenewswire.com/en/news-release/2023/04/06/2642270/0/en/AI-in-Education-Market-Size-To-Reach-USD-23-82-Billion-by-2030-with-a-CAGR-of-38-Report-by-Market-Research-Future-MRFR.html

Gurtu, A. (2021, June 2). Five industries reaping the benefits of artificial intelligence. *Forbes*. https://www.forbes.com/sites/forbestechcouncil/2021/06/02/five-industries-reaping-the-benefits-of-artificial-intelligence/?sh=613eddd559ca

Harvey, D., Lobban, F., Rayson, P., Warner, A., & Jones, S. (2022, April). Natural language processing methods and bipolar disorder: Scoping review. *JMIR Mental Health*, 9(4). https://mental.jmir.org/2022/4/e35928

Holmes, W., Bialik, M., & Fadel, C. (2019). *Artificial intelligence in education*. Independent. https://repository.globethics.net/handle/20.500.12424/4276068

Hu, X., Cirit, O., Binaykiya, T., & Hora, R. (2022, February 10). DeepETA: How Uber predicts arrival times using deep learning. *Uber Blog*. https://www.uber.com/blog/deepeta-how-uber-predicts-arrival-times

Johnson, A. (2023, September 12). Which jobs will AI replace? These 4 industries will be heavily impacted. *Forbes*. https://www.forbes.com/sites/ariannajohnson/2023/03/30/which-jobs-will-ai-replace-these-4-industries-will-be-heavily-impacted

Julien. (2019, June 11). 7 ways you are already using artificial intelligence daily. *Bocasay*. https://www.bocasay.com/7-ways-using-artificial-intelligence

Keierlber, M. (2022, April 21). This teen shared her trouble with a robot. Could AI "chatbots" solve the youth mental health crisis? *LA School Report*. https://www.laschoolreport.com/this-teen-shared-her-troubles-with-a-robot-could-ai-chatbots-solve-the-youth-mental-health-crisis

Kennedy, S. (2022, April 26). Natural language processing can improve bipolar care. *Health IT Analytics/TechTarget*. https://healthitanalytics.com/news/natural-language-processing-can-improve-bipolar-disorder-care

Kessler, S. (2023, June 10). The A.I. revolution will change work. Nobody agrees how. *New York Times*. https://www.nytimes.com/2023/06/10/business/ai-jobs-work.html

Kochhar, R. (2023, July 26). Which U.S. workers are more exposed to AI on their jobs? *Pew Research Center*. https://www.pewresearch.org/social-trends/2023/07/26/which-u-s-workers-are-more-exposed-to-ai-on-their-jobs

Krishan, A. (2023, April 17). Federal gov spending on AI hit $3.3b in fiscal 2022: Study. *FedScoop*. https://fedscoop.com/us-spending-on-ai-hit-3-3b-in-fiscal-2022

Lagatta, E. (2023, August 20). Are you smarter than a robot? Study finds bots better than us at passing CAPTCHA tests. *USA Today*. https://www.usatoday.com/story/tech/2023/08/17/captcha-tests-keep-more-humans-than-bots-out-study-shows/70609691007

Lee, I., & Perret, B. (2022, June). Preparing high school teachers to integrate AI methods into STEM classrooms. *Proceedings of the AAAI Conference on Artificial Intelligence*, 36(11), 1278312–791. https://doi.org/10.1609/aaai.v36i11.21557

Lynch, M. (2021, August 17). Is artificial intelligence the future of education? *Education Week*. https://blogs.edweek.org/edweek/education_futures/2017/08/is_artificial_intelligence_the_future_of_education.html

McClennen, N., & Poth, R. D. (2022, December 16). Education is about to radically change: AI for the masses. *Getting Smart*. https://www.gettingsmart.com/2022/12/16/education-is-about-to-radically-change-ai-for-the-masses

McFarland, A. (2023, November 20). 10 best AI tools for education. *Unite.AI*. https://www.unite.ai/10-best-ai-tools-for-education

Nagel, D. (2023, January 1). AI to experience massive growth in education. *THE Journal*. https://thejournal.com/articles/2023/01/12/ai-to-experience-massive-growth-in-education.aspx

Napolitano, E. (2023, June 2). AI eliminated nearly 4,000 jobs in May, report says. *CBS News*. https://www.cbsnews.com/news/ai-job-losses-artificial-intelligence-challenger-report

Ortiz, S. (2023, August 18). 40% of workers will have to reskill in the next three years due to AI, says IBM study. *ZD Net*. https://www.zdnet.com/article/40-of-workers-will-have-to-reskill-in-the-next-three-years-due-to-ai-says-ibm-study

Patel, N. (2023, October 17). Clearview AI and the end of privacy, with author Kashmir Hill. *The Verge*. https://www.theverge.com/23919134/kashmir-hill-your-face-belongs-to-us-clearview-ai-facial-recognition-privacy-decoder

Quizlet. (2023, March 1). Quizlet launches "Q-Chat" AI tutor built with OpenAI API. *PR Newswire*. https://www.prnewswire.com/news-releases/quizlet-launches-q-chat-ai-tutor-built-with-openai-api-301759014.html

Restaurant Engine. (2024). *How many customers use mobile devices to find restaurants?* https://restaurantengine.com/how-many-customers-use-mobile-devices-to-find-restaurants

Roth, E. (2023, December 27). The *New York Times* is suing OpenAI and Microsoft for copyright infringement. *The Verge*. https://www.theverge.com/2023/12/27/24016212/new-york-times-openai-microsoft-lawsuit-copyright-infringement

S, R. K., & George, S. (2020, September 21). Why skills—not degrees—will shape the future of work. *World Economic Forum*. https://www.weforum.org/agenda/2020/09/reckoning-for-skills

Sauer, M. (2022, May 12). Mark Cuban predicts AI will dominate the future workplace: To be successful, "you're going to have to understand it." *Make It*. https://www.cnbc.com/2022/05/12/why-mark-cuban-predicts-ai-will-dominate-the-future-workplace.html

Sierra, S. (2023, December 28). AG Bonta called to investigate Clearview AI for allegedly selling images to police without consent. *abc7News*. https://abc7news.com/clearview-ai-california-attorney-general-rob-bonta-consumer-watchdog/14231840

Simon, C. (2022, June 28). Council post: As AI advances, will human workers disappear? *Forbes*. https://www.forbes.com/sites/forbestechcouncil/2022/06/28/as-ai-advances-will-human-workers-disappear

Sirohi, N. (2019, May 25). Artificial intelligence: An explainer for beginners. *The Leaflet*. https://theleaflet.in/artificial-intelligence-an-explainer-for-beginners

Study.com. (2023, February 1). *ChatGPT in the classroom.* https://study.com/resources/chatgpt-in-the-classroom#:~:text=43%25%20of%20teachers%20think%20ChatGPT,should%20be%20banned%20in%20schools

Touretzky, D., Gardner-McCune, C., Breazeal, C., Martin, F., & Seehorn, D. (2019, December 1). A year in k–12 AI education. *AI Magazine, 40*(4), 88–90. https://doi.org/10.1609/aimag.v40i4.5289

Trust, T., & Maloy, R. W. (2023, September 22). Learning about civics and government: The ethics of AI in political campaigns. *Learning as I Go: Reflections & Lessons Learned, Rachelle Dené Poth.* https://rdene915.com/2023/09/22/learning-about-civics-and-government-the-ethics-of-ai-in-political-campaigns

Trust, T., Whalen, J., & Mouza, C. (2023). Editorial: ChatGPT: Challenges, opportunities, and implications for teacher education. *Contemporary Issues and Technology in Teacher Education, 23*(1), 1–23. https://www.learntechlib.org/primary/p/222408

U.S. Department of Education Office of Educational Technology. (2023, May 24). *Artificial intelligence and the future of teaching and learning.* https://tech.ed.gov/ai-future-of-teaching-and-learning

Watters, A. (2023, January 13). 30+ artificial intelligence statistics and facts for 2023. *CompTIA.* https://connect.comptia.org/blog/artificial-intelligence-statistics-facts

Wdadmin. (2018, May 17). Teaching AI for K–12 students: National guidelines. *Center for Neural Basis for Cognition.* https://www.cnbc.cmu.edu/2018/05/17/teaching-ai-for-k-12-students-national-guidelines

The White House. (2023, October 30). *Fact sheet: President Biden issues executive order on safe, secure, and trustworthy artificial intelligence.* https://www.whitehouse.gov/briefing-room/statements-releases/2023/10/30/fact-sheet-president-biden-issues-executive-order-on-safe-secure-and-trustworthy-artificial-intelligence

Wiggers, K. (2023, September 21). The copyright issues around generative AI aren't going away anytime soon. *Tech Crunch.* https://techcrunch.com/2023/09/21/the-copyright-issues-around-generative-ai-arent-going-away-anytime-soon

Wilson, N. (2022, March 1). Winston-Salem students work with first A.I. woman of color. *Fox8 News.* https://myfox8.com/news/north-carolina/winston-salem/winston-salem-students-work-with-first-a-i-woman-of-color

Wodecki, B. (2023, November 21). Leaderboard: OpenAI's GPT-4 has lowest hallucination rate. *AI Business.* https://aibusiness.com/nlp/openai-s-gpt-4-surpasses-rivals-in-document-summary-accuracy

World Economic Forum. (2020, January). *Jobs of tomorrow: Mapping opportunity in the new economy.* https://www.weforum.org/reports/jobs-of-tomorrow-mapping-opportunity-in-the-new-economy

World Economic Forum. (2023, April 30). *Future of jobs report 2023: Up to a quarter of jobs expected to change in next five years.* https://www.weforum.org/press/2023/04/future-of-jobs-report-2023-up-to-a-quarter-of-jobs-expected-to-change-in-next-five-years?

Zinkula, J. (2024, January 10). 4 careers where workers will have to change jobs by 2030 due to AI and shifts in how we shop, a McKinsey study says. *Business Insider.* https://www.businessinsider.com/jobs-at-risk-from-ai-replace-change-chatgpt-automation-study-2023-7

Index

www.ingramcontent.com/pod-product-compliance
Lightning Source LLC
Chambersburg PA
CBHW080841120626
46553CB00009B/2515